Matters of Feeling:

Values Education Reconsidered

by

Joseph S. Junell

Central Washington State University

A Publication of the Phi Delta Kappa Educational Foundation

Cover design by Victoria Voelker

© 1979 Joseph S. Junell
All rights reserved
Library of Congress Catalog Card Number 79-54645
ISBN 0-87367-421-9
Printed in the United States of America

Dedication

To Stanley Elam, who believed that this book might have something of value for educators and whose unflagging encouragement gently prodded me on to its completion.

Also to my wife Bernice, who understood better than anyone else how important it was to me that I finish it.

Contents

Preface

This book is an attempt to explore the teaching of values as it is conducted in our public schools today. It briefly examines the philosophy underlying such efforts, as well as some of the confusion and ignorance that pervade so much of this teaching.

It also offers a specific point of view, with some hint at practical applications. In doing so, it takes issue with the popular concept that values can be taught through the methods of logical analysis and science, which involve such techniques as *values clarification, moral dilemmas,* and the like. It argues that values, to the degree that schools can teach them at all, can be taught only through emotionally related processes of *identification* and through the arts of persuasion and drama. Unlike scientific methods, these approaches admittedly place considerable restrictions on the child's field of choice.

The traditional inability of schools to impose such restrictions has a disturbing corollary in the fact that, as academic performance declines and discipline problems increase, more and more highly qualified teachers are bowing out of the profession. The problem is not necessarily one of money. Actually, teacher salaries compare reasonably well with those of professional middle-class wage earners. The problem, rather, is the teacher's growing doubts about his ability to make a difference. He is finding that Thoreau's statement about students who march to a different drummer is far more a literary virtue than a real one. And when, year after year, fewer and fewer students keep time with his beat, he begins to wonder if his drumming is all that bad, or if children are becoming academically and socially tone deaf. He knows that social and academic fulfillment can only come out of a powerful alliance between school and society, but everywhere about him he sees this alliance in a state of decay, if indeed it ever existed.

In pursuing this theme, and others, I often find myself in the unenviable position of having to defend what appears to be an inflexible code that needs to be transmitted intact from generation to generation. I plead guilty. I am aware of the risk in holding rigidly to a tradition or creed; too often its promise of comfort and security turns out to be dangerously false. Nor am I against the examination of any value through rational processes, especially as it may be, and often is, influenced by other factors. For example, although dignity is a characteristic often found among members of undeveloped nations, equality is far less common. Often described as an inalienable right, equality has depended heavily upon a society living in the lap of abundance.

Nevertheless, down through the ages, those traditions or absolutes that were translated into specific modes of behavior have played a vital role in the continuation of the species. We might suspect that primitive man found his environment singularly mystifying and hostile. Only a few things could be trusted to recur without fail: a stone thrown into the air invariably fell; a piece of wood floated. For the most part there was little he could depend on. A calm day was shattered by a devastating storm; a season of plenty was followed by one of starvation. These, and similar events, were undoubtedly a constant source of terror and threat, for they struck without warning or without known cause.

Into such an alien world primitive man found his way, equipped like other animals with certain primary drives necessary for survival, but with one notable exception: Survival behaviors among lower animals were instinctive, thus eliminating much of the terrible burden of conflict and stress resulting from the lack of predictability. Man had to *learn* such survival behaviors. To assuage this fear of the unpredictable, which many social scientists believe stems from a genetically based craving for order, he began slowly and painfully, over countless generations, to rearrange the meaningless universe that at first puzzled and terrified him. With infinite patience he manipulated and reshaped his natural surroundings. Out of subjective experience he created vast and complicated systems of thought.

Man's traditions, as a reflection of the ceaseless task of attributing causes, of devising laws to explain the inexplicable, began to take on a unique role. They were like familiar guideposts enabling him to walk at ease in a world that was largely unfamiliar and frightening. True, they limited his choice of response, but they also soothed his tensions and fear of the unknown.

Uncertainty wears on the nerves. It leads, as Pavlov's experiments have shown, to mental exhaustion and insanity. To protect himself, man built a great hierarchy of traditions covering everything from religious belief to property rights. These resembled the working hypotheses in the scientist's experiments, and on to them he pinned his hopes that, eight or so times out of 10, perhaps, they would give him the right answers.

Nor did right answers necessarily have to be true. It was enough, as reknowned anthropologist Bronislaw Malinowski has pointed out, that they achieved among the populace "mental integration, optimism, and confidence," that they "established organization, led to courage, endurance, and perseverance," and finally involved all members of a society in the work of providing for the common good. It is little wonder that any contradiction to them, whether founded on fact or fiction, was frequently regarded as a threat to security and indeed to life itself.

It is really not my purpose to recommend what values should be taught, or whether they should be taught at all, but rather to show how schools may to a degree duplicate the process by which values are internalized from infancy on up. Everything that I have read or observed nags at me and tells me that this process is one that involves severe limitation rather than a wide range of choice in stimuli and response. As a natural consequence, it cannot but help evoke from some quarters cries of dogma, demagoguery, and indoctrination.

If so, there is no help for it. Every game we play in life is a game of chance in which the odds against winning or losing must be taken into account. Learning how to improve the odds becomes a matter of enormous significance. For any game that attempts to perpetuate our democratic ideals may well be the most important one we will ever play. Moreover, it is a never-ending game, played by generation after generation.

As I see it, there is only one way to play it successfully—which happens to be the subject of this book.

Joseph S. Junell
July, 1979

One

Is Rational Man Our First Priority?

The report card for mankind reads: A in physics. B or B- in genetics. C or D in psychology. F in morality, ethics, and the humanities.[1]

—Ben Brodinsky

There is a scene in *David Copperfield* (one of the few novels I have read several times) that fills me with a sense of pathos I would ordinarily admit to only with considerable embarrassment. It is the scene in which David, after a series of cruel experiences, escapes from London and confronts his aunt, Betsey Trotwood, who has not seen him since the day of his birth. Standing before her, a dirty, ragged, underfed, and shockingly misused child of 10, he pleads that he be accepted into her household. The scene is filled with all the outrageous sentimentality of which Dickens is master. Yet I cannot return to David's words without that familiar rush of absurd feelings.

"I am David Copperfield of Blunderstone, in Suffolk—where you came on the night when I was born and saw my dear mama. I have been unhappy since she died. I have been slighted and taught nothing, and thrown upon myself, and put to work not fit for me. It has made me run away to you. I was robbed at first setting out, and have walked all the way, and have never slept in a bed since I began the journey." Here my self-support gave way all at once, and, with a movement of my hands, intended to show my ragged state, and call it to witness that I suffered something, I broke into a passion of crying, which I suppose had been pent up within me all the week.

During the while, I experience all of David's tensions and emotions. His tears are my tears, for I, too, have suffered the calculated horror of the Murdstones, the educational process at Salem House that was next to sheer brutality, and the grim evils of the child's workhouse in London.

I do not pretend that this reaction to Dickens has shaped all my thinking about education, child labor, or the forces of evil and good; other impressions have long since helped round out the pic-

1

ture. But I should be dishonest if I did not confess that these emotional journeys with David, along with many, many others, have done much to forge the attitudes and feelings that are primary to my system of values, and that they influence many of my thoughts and decisions with the force of conviction.

Assuming that Dickens was dealing with distinctive behaviors still fundamental to moral conduct, it is interesting that the most significant contributions to public education made in the past two decades have had little of importance to say about the unique relationship of emotion and identification to school curriculum and its consequent impact on survival. Men like Jerome Bruner and B. F. Skinner—top names in education today—are pursuing their own private visions of the ideal. Although they appear to be traveling along different pathways, it is the same lodestar that attracts them; namely, the deification of the rational-scientific processes as a means of coping with problems that humans are now facing on a global scale. In concert with their efforts, and often as a result of them, every modern innovation, from school architecture to computerized learning, helps usher in full scale this glittering, gem-hard analytic age. The response to Lord Whitehead's dictum that the nation is doomed which does not place value on trained intelligence has been taken up with a vengeance.

Nor are present-day academicians espousing this view hard to find. In a provocative essay review of Arthur Schlesinger's book, *The Crisis of Confidence: Ideas, Power and Violence in America,*[2] John Bunzel, president of San Jose State College, raises by implication the most nagging of all questions with which educators, since the days of Socrates, have ineffectually come to grips: To what part of man does public education owe its first obligation? Is it to his intellectual-academic world, or his emotional-social one? Which is more likely to insure him a measure of happiness and a reasonable chance of survival?

As with most scholars throughout America, Bunzel's position on this matter hardly comes as a surprise. For both himself and Schlesinger, the art of reflection is the only antidote to the insanity that daily encroaches upon our democratic way of life, as well as upon the world at large. Like Schlesinger, Bunzel "gives no quarter to those who would reject the process of reason" for the "simple ladling out of moral judgments."[3] He quotes the professor who insists that a "spectrum of opinion and action is indispensable if reason is to civilize power" and abjures within youth the "change in life-style which locates its center in a bewildering grab bag of sources that includes hallucinatory drugs and Eastern mystics, encounter groups and communal pads—in short, in the sense and emotions." Along with Schlesinger, his concern "is not simply the impulse to irrationalism that is evident everywhere but the abandonment of rationality as a way to help set things right. . . . A liberal," he goes on to say, "does not deny or minimize the destructive tendencies that are a part of man's irrational component; rather, he reasserts the conviction that irrational motivations can best be treated at the conscious level, where they can be exposed to reason."[4]

Certainly there is much in Bunzel's words that compels admiration and a high level of agreement. There is also a certain naiveté to which historians are particularly prone. This naiveté is reflected in the belief that "reason" truly civilizes power, that "irrational motivations" are best corrected by exposing them to reason, or that "man's irrational component" is primarily destructive in nature. It is especially evident in the implication that the reasoning process can be trained to function objectively without the intervention of the senses and emotions.

Such indomitable faith in the powers of the mind to solve any problem, however complex, can only be explained within the context of history. Its roots, as we know, are found in the age of rationalism, created by the extraordinary impact of ideas of such men as Copernicus, Kepler, Galileo, Newton, and Descartes. It was a world in which reason for the first time tried to provide "rational" controls for individual and social life, and in general to discard or minimize notions that were merely venerable, traditional, unproved, or irrational. To a large extent Montaigne abandoned his quest for absolute truth and advanced instead the virtues of doubt and tolerance. Bacon set his seal on inductive reasoning, and Descartes devoted himself to the task of reshaping philosophy into a pattern consistent with the new science. Among the learned it was a period of much optimism and hope, with a strong belief in rationality striking the central chord.

The movement did not progress without periods of strong reaction, of which the anti-intellectualism of Rousseau and Bergson are cases in point. Rousseau's concept of the noble savage, for example, is strongly reminiscent of much that we witnessed in American society no more than a decade ago, as is also his rejection of reason in favor of conscience and feeling as the only true guides to correct moral and social behavior. Bergson's extravagances regarding the superiority of instinct and intuition over intellect are only slightly less well-known.

In spite of such minor reverses, knowledge as end product has so permeated the educational process that even the old charges of anti-intellectualism against John Dewey by such critics as Arthur Bestor, John Maynard Hutchins, and others seem in retrospect a little absurd. Richard Hofstader's dim view of the child-centered school portrayed in his *Anti-intellectualism in*

American Life,[5] for example, is a brilliant piece of logic, but I cannot believe that this is the part of Dewey that continues to influence the schools of today. When theorists like Bruner talk about the discovery of "structure" in the teaching of mathematics and science, when Edwin Fenton speaks of the coming revolution in the social studies through problem solving, inquiry learning, and other inductive approaches, they borrow directly or indirectly from the opposite side of Dewey revealed through one of his less well-known but far more pervasive volumes, *How We Think,* published in 1933.[6] Advancing the method of scientific inquiry as representative of the most highly sophisticated of all intellectual processes, it soon became education's first definitive handbook for implementing pragmatic philosophy. Moreover, it was a testament of Dewey's faith in what he believed to be the virtually limitless power of human intelligence.

Meanwhile, the other adjuncts of Dewey's belief—learning as social function, to take an instance—that imply at least a modicum of concern with moral behavior, have been either relegated to the limbo of lip service or so overshadowed by the intellectual aspects of learning as to remain for all practical purposes totally defunct. Nowhere is this truth more ironically pointed up than in the learner upon whom Dewey pinned his loftiest hopes: the elementary school child. Enter any classroom and place the subjects—citizenship among them—in random order on the chalkboard. Then ask the children, as I have done on various occasions, to rearrange them anonymously according to their importance. Citizenship is sure to receive short shrift, for invariably it will appear among the other classroom pariahs—music, physical education, and art—at the bottom of the list.

This does not mean that small children enjoy these subjects less; it means simply that, in matters of assigning value, they quickly adopt the attitudes of the school and society which mete out their punishment and rewards and whose demands have been made quite plain. In a large survey reported by the *Review of Educational Research* in the early Sixties, several thousand respondents—predominantly educators—pointed out what they expect of elementary schools in the way of purposes and functions. The school's task, they felt, was not the teaching of social living. It was identified, first with the three Rs and, second, with "the cultivation of a love of knowledge."[7] Nearly 10 years later a survey conducted by the Gallup Organization for the Charles F. Kettering Foundation revealed essentially the same picture. The elementary equivalents of the humanities received rock-bottom ratings. Social living was not even mentioned.[8] Today the vast

4

ongoing shift in emphasis from traditional to discovery type programs, plus the addition of new disciplines, makes it clear that the prevailing view of the school's proper function is an academic one. This is one lesson even the dullest child learns rapidly—and sometimes painfully—on the very first day he brings home his report card.

Whether we can attribute the whole of the intellectual movement dominating elementary education to Dewey's theorizing about the nature of scientific inquiry is of course doubtful; other factors have exerted powerful influences. But there can be no doubt of Dewey's impact on what Joseph Wood Krutch calls the "modern proponents of 'scientific' morality" who insist that "value judgments should be based on knowledge rather than tradition or intuition,"[9] nor of the stifling effect this view has had on any sort of value teaching that is not analytically oriented. I know of no experiment approaching the scale of the open concept classroom, for example, designed to inculcate through processes involving feeling and emotion the abiding values that have historically motivated our brightest moments in social and political development or, conversely, that are calculated to give emotional awareness to those periods of national shame when men callously laid these values aside.

It is this vital process, often called vicarious experience, that has been conspicuously absent from the elementary curriculum at a stage in the child's development when he is most susceptible to its influence. My complaint is not that school people engaged in teaching, writing, and editing of instructional materials refuse to juggle facts dishonestly for the sake of dramatizing them, but that they fail to dramatize facts or events even when to do so is historically legitimate. Many facets of the social sciences, as well as the language arts, abound in rivalries, danger, and conflict containing strong moral issues charged with emotional content. These make fertile soil for the development of primary social values, values terribly important to the survival of the race. Unfortunately for small children, they seldom see the light of day. Too often they are neglected in favor of a bland diet of flawless expository writing. Sometimes they are suppressed or omitted because of opinionated ideas about emotional readiness or because of current fetishes regarding concept building, problem solving, and other such panaceas. Meanwhile, the most promising techniques of drama and commitment to basic emotional appeal go begging, slowly getting buried under a mountain of new "discovery" oriented programs.

Whatever the faults of the *McGuffey Reader*, it did represent a consciously conceived plan for *dramatizing* the values most important to the society that lived before the turn of the century. No doubt many of them, once considered imperishable laws of conduct, have long since disappeared under the press of changing times. Yet, as one humanities professor of my acquaintance argued about the *Reader:* "It was archaic in style, sentimental, heavy with moralistic platitudes, yes. Unrealistic, no. The idea was unique, for it assumed, as so many educators and curriculum writers today refrain from doing, that morality was as much a part of real life as arithmetic, science, or technology."

It is curious that social scientists are just now beginning to learn through experimentation what men of letters have known intuitively for centuries. "Some evidence indicates," Gordon Allport tells us in his book *The Nature of Prejudice,* "that films, novels, dramas may be effective, presumably because they induce identification.... If this finding stands up in future research, we shall be confronted with an interesting possibility.... Perhaps in the future we shall decide that intercultural programs should *start* [italics Allport's] with fiction, drama, and films, and move gradually into more realistic methods of training."[10] I once wrote the editor of a popular journal that the real tragedy in avoiding the controversial issues of history is not that it perverts truth but that it destroys the single most powerful medium, apart from fiction, that enables children to relive at concert pitch the moral and spiritual conflicts of the race. Several years ago the gifted novelist Norman Mailer told his reading audience that he had set for himself a task no less arduous than that of reshaping America's conscience. An ambitious undertaking. How much simpler to start out fresh with small children!

Making sense out of what values to teach, when to teach them, and under what conditions they should be taught has been equally affected by the new spirit of scientific intellectualism. When recently I asked my class of aspiring young teachers if they believed there were principles of behavior so fundamental as to warrant having them taught to all children without benefit of validating evidence or majority consensus, they were plainly disturbed. There was fear that unanimity of acceptance could lead only to the evils of conformity. They wondered if values should be the same for everyone. After all, they argued, we do live in a highly pluralistic society. When I inquired if they meant by this that pluralism was an ideal state of affairs, they demurred by saying, "Why not? It's been a primary source of our strength for a couple of hundred years now. Besides, does anyone have the right to tell people what values they should live by? Isn't this really a form of indoctrination?"

Although my answer to the last two questions was an unconditional "yes," I profess my inability to base it on any sort of "knowledge." To the first question I can reply only according to the dictates of my own system of values, forged, I suppose, by humanist principles and by the sum total of experiences unique to me. These suggest strongly that certain democratic values seem to be the common heritage of all men of all times and of all conditions, and that a better way must be explored to transmit them intact to all children of future generations. This is not to say that their appearance among men is of the same nature as Plato's ideas—those shadowy entities that pass eternally between some "otherworld" and their human habitations. Rather, they are the very special product of man's biological and psychological drives, singularly reflective of a particular stage in his evolutionary development. Put into Skinnerian terms, they are those "behaviors which have proved reinforcing as a result of the genetic endowment of the organism and of the nature of its environment."[11] As such they have been embraced, I venture to say, at some time, in some form, and to some degree by humans everywhere. Under the tyrant's heel they have undergone suppression and suffered extinction. As ideals they have never enjoyed the promise of complete fulfillment, and perhaps never will. Yet, I submit that they are unique urgings for which man has ceaselessly hungered throughout the long and troubled course of human history.

These selfsame urgings also suggest that value teaching is abominable when it becomes a double standard—when, as in so many classrooms during the Vietnam War, for example, it preached reverence and dignity for human life, on the one hand, and endorsed, on the other, the development of a sophisticated rationale for the maiming and slaughter of thousands of innocent children in the prosecution of a "minor holding action." Indeed, for schools to encourage any kind of intellectual discourse that tries to synthesize or rationalize these antithetical positions constitutes hypocrisy of monstrous proportions.

As to the second question, if by indoctrination is meant the instilling of beliefs without the benefit of alternatives or substantiation by facts, my answer, again, is simply that the values I hold most significant are those least supportable by empirical data. While it would not be terribly important if the reverse were true, it is comforting to know that no less profound a thinker than the late Bertrand Russell in some part shared this view. "There remains," he tells us, "a vast field where scientific methods are inadequate. This field includes the ultimate questions of value; science alone, for example, cannot prove that it is bad to enjoy the infliction of cruelty. Whatever can be known, can be known by means of science, but things which are legitimately matters of feeling lie outside its province."[12]

Unfortunately, many educators and curriculum writers seem only dimly aware that "things which are legitimately matters of feeling" are perhaps best taught through methods which involve feeling and that the style and emphasis of such writing and teaching are quite different from those designed to teach children how to discover, assimilate, and use information. With regard to the problem of making decisions, the child is trained in the art of critically examining his facts and acting upon them in a manner that leaves open for him the widest range of options for achieving his goal. This is an intellectual process in which the method of scientific inquiry is admittedly a powerful tool. In the case of emotions, attitudes, or feelings, the process is diametrically opposite. Basically, it is a *prior* function. Its sole purpose is to insure the internalization of specific attitudes and values by which goals are screened through a kind of moral retina, as it were. Here, options are severely limited, and to insist, as the new breed of educator often does, that elements of "choice," "inquiry," "operational truth," and the like are fundamental strategies in creating this moral synthesis is as naive as to assume that once children have "discovered" the truth about drugs the problem will cease to exist.

What makes far more sense to me is the theory advanced by Freud and his followers. At the risk of oversimplification, it tells us that the moral component is born and developed, for better or for worse, within a uniquely emotional climate that includes, among other things, a *systematic*—though not necessarily planned—weighting of the scale in terms of exposure to prescribed beliefs and behaviors. By means of a principle Freud chose to call identification, children internalize such beliefs and behaviors in order to integrate disassociated elements of their own personalities. The process is completely self-actuated, apparently resulting from a profound need for stability and a sense of order.

In one respect, if in no other, the theories of behaviorists such as Skinner are somewhat alike in that desirable behavior—or rather those beliefs that motivate desirable behavior—is deemed to be the product of conditioning techniques in which *design*, either conscious or unconscious, is a crucial factor. More specifically, it may be described as a condition in which selectively reinforced and reinforcing responses to selected stimuli have been found to be consistent with both the organism's biological needs and the social norms under which he lives. Although the Freudian view of value formation to me appears the more fruitful approach, for reasons I shall later discuss, I see them both as having complementary functions in the classroom; indeed, Freudian and behaviorist principles are interwoven in ways that are difficult, if not impossible, to separate.

Having said this, I wish to emphasize that I shall not address myself to the obvious questions: "Whose values shall we teach?" or "Is value teaching really the proper function of our schools?" Consensus on such questions must be arrived at through the democratic process. Meanwhile, it may be safely stated that *something* in the way of attitude and value formation is occurring in classrooms throughout America, but for reasons that few of us can define or to what end almost none of us can predict. Indeed, some proponents of values clarification, the accepted scientifically oriented technique for modifying values, regard these aspects of unpredictability and lack of control as democratic virtues, since the group decisions of autonomous men and women always contain elements of uncertainty. There is little evidence to show, however, that these outcomes, whatever they happen to be, exert greater influence in strengthening our democratic institutions and beliefs than they do in reinforcing the extremes of pluralism that now so cruelly divide society at large.

I am aware that the directions I advocate (primarily for young children) strike terror in some hearts, for they smack ominously of conditioning and indoctrination. And there is in fact a sense in which conditioned allegiance to values is predominantly absolute and irreversible. If the emotions are deeply involved, as they almost always are, allegiance becomes especially imperious and demanding, a jealous mistress who brooks no trifling with the claims of rival beliefs. Even more disturbing, the condition often poses at one and the same time the alternate paths of survival and extinction. Few have pointed out more dramatically than Bronislaw Malinowski the survival value of taboo in primitive cultures, where the social and economic life of the populace is reasonably stabilized. When stability is threatened, however, powerfully induced modes of behavior become virtual deathtraps, bringing down the curtain on more than one society, including many among our own Indian tribes.

I suppose that considerations like these have to some degree caused educators to look askance at all educational systems leading to rigid belief. Any system, however, that attempts to strike a compromise between the philosophies of unbridled freedom and totalitarianism must take a calculated risk, and I, for one, would rather see that risk taken on the side of what appears to me to be man's predominant genetic tendencies to behavior; namely, that he is primarily a creature of emotion, that his adherence to reason in the role of decision making is more figment than fact, and that his philosophies are far more the product of his ego needs than his ego needs are the image of his philosophies. What powers of reason he does possess, however, are among his most unique attributes and are not to be underestimated. But unless he is taught early in life to use these powers in support of a few strongly and emotionally conditioned attitudes and beliefs to which all men can accede, his presence on earth will continue to grow steadily more uncertain.

If such an emphasis on my part indicates a kind of perverse blindness to the virtues of scientific intellectualism, well and good. I am far less concerned that our children learn to create new values in a changing world than I am about their ability to safeguard and perpetuate a few of what Sir Herbert Read has called the "great simplicities" that touch the deepest springs in human relationships. At the same time, I do not see how they can serve mankind except as a great hierarchy of universals whose demands upon all alike are exacting and immutable. It is significant that the late Clyde Kluckhohn, a noted anthropologist who spent the greater part of his productive years describing the incredible diversity that marks human cultures, should have written near the end of his life: "[A]ll talk of an eventual peaceful and orderly world is but pious cant or sentimental fantasy unless there are, in fact, some simple but powerful things in which all men can believe, some codes or canons that have or can obtain universal acceptance."[13] It is upon our commitment to these and the successful teaching of them that all civilizations, if they are to survive, must ultimately rest.

In further pursuing this theme, I find it necessary to point out that it is no more my intent to discredit the need for reason than it is to elevate the position of emotions. I argue strictly in terms of priorities—what *must* come first, rather than what is of greater or lesser importance. My thesis is simply that because attitudes function in the peculiar way they do, the emotions of young children must be made the primary target of public education, and the educator who wishes to improve the human condition without full recognition of this fact is merely whistling in the dark. He must be able to distinguish between attitudes that are liberating and those that are imprisoning; between the ones that most fully enable the child's imagination to range free and those that slam the door shut on him, so that often he stands outside it, not even wondering what lies beyond. The educator must be made to realize that the imprisoned mind is, in some respects, as much the product of Scarsdale as it is of Harlem, and that college credentials are by no means a guarantee against it. As we shall note in succeeding chapters, he must have some inkling, finally, of these factors most likely to influence attitudes, as well as some understanding of the many ramifications—both significant and unpleasant—closely related to this process.

Two

Truth and Consequences

I am persuaded that this intoxication [generated by the pragmatist concept of "truth"] is the greatest danger of our time, and that any philosophy which, however unintentionally, contributes to it is increasing the danger of vast social disaster.[14]

—*Lord Bertrand Russell*

Granting that personal rectitude and commitment to a few ideals still occupy a position of some importance in human affairs, it is perhaps not irrelevant to ask how well equipped is the new teacher to deal with them in the classroom. The outlook at first glance is most promising. The young teachers who are coming out of our colleges and universities now form a new and distinctive class of men and women. Urbane, generous, and knowledgeable, their collective presence is being felt throughout the land. They were once fed on watered-down courses, frills, and general academic pap. Now there are demands for quantity and quality in content. A growing respect for empiricism and research is turning young prospective teachers into devotees of tough-minded intellectualism. They know facts about perception and its relationship to learning that were still mysteries 20 years ago. Their understanding of the problems of youth, though by no means complete, has increased enormously in the past decade. They are responsible, dedicated, and sympathetic. Armed with the knowledge and new techniques of science, they are becoming skilled practitioners who promise to revolutionize education from top to bottom.

Unfortunately, upon closer examination, the brightness of this promise starts to fade. There is, to begin with, the plain fact of confused objectives. My own experience as an observer in hundreds of classrooms has convinced me that while teachers often profess to be dealing with values, they are seldom sure of what they are teaching or to what purpose. The judgment is not mine alone. Theodore Brameld, for years the leading proponent of reconstructionism in educational philosophy, has conceded on at least one occasion that "[O]ur schools and colleges, by and large,

11

are neither consistent nor clear about the values they are obliged to instill in the young.... Insofar as American education has tended to regard its chief business as that of conveying information and training in skills, it has tended to store its values, so to speak, in the educational attic."[15]

Even more damaging is research evidence on the changing values of the new teacher. Brief excerpts from two surveys of the literature are worthy of review. The first of these, by the psychologist Jacob W. Getzels, reports the findings from four major studies conducted by the University of Chicago. According to Getzels, they reveal an unmistakable drift among college students (teachers included) from a traditional, hard-nosed value orientation to a shifting, quixotic pattern that social scientists have come to call "the emergent values." "The goal of behavior is not personal rectitude but group consensus, not originality but adjustment." Great importance has been placed on "an overriding value of sociability and frictionless interpersonal relations" in which "the hard-working self-determined Horatio Alger hero is giving way to the affable young man in the gray flannel suit." Taking the place of "Puritan morality or...moral commitment, as a value, there are relativistic moral attitudes without strong personal commitments. Absolutes in right or wrong are questionable. In a sense, morality has become a statistical, rather than an ethical, concept; morality is what the group thinks is moral."[16]

The second survey, by W. W. Charters, Jr., corroborates most of Getzels's findings, but its principal virtue lies in a summary of the work of George Spindler, the Stanford anthropologist. Unlike Getzels, Spindler worked in the realm of hypothesis. Vast industrial expansion, he reasoned, plus two global wars and a turbulent social history, had all but eroded the traditional values of a former agrarian society. The last citadel of moral respectability, the work-success ethic, and the hard-line traditional value system, was to be found in the middle and lower-middle classes. It is from these classes that the vast majority of America's teachers are drawn. The influence of teacher training institutions, however, is clearly in the direction of emergent values. The result has been to create "ambivalence" and "vacillation" among some young teachers and to drive others to the extremes of rigid "authoritarianism" on the one hand, or the "group-think" cult of social adjustment on the other. A third teacher, whom Spindler calls the adaptive teacher, follows a pattern similar to those described, but in far less severe form.

To date I know of no research that would prove that Spindler's teachers do indeed follow these patterns of behavior. However, Charters does cite a number of studies to show that the new teacher reflects "such emergent values as sociability, a relativistic moral attitude, consideration of others, conformity to the group, and a hedonistic present-time orientation."[17]

Whatever the teachers' personal beliefs and feelings about relativism, there can be little doubt of their commitment to the philosophy that engenders it. A system of thought that regards hierarchy and permanence as questionable virtues logically points to the application of empiricism in value teaching. Thus when you suggest to this young teacher that scientific methods are by no means a cure-all for society's ailments or that there is need to pass on to future generations a body of fixed values, he will smile indulgently and ask: "Whose values? Yours or mine?" This is tantamount to saying, of course, that the importance of any particular value is largely a matter of personal preference and that what is one man's meat may well be another man's poison. Models for this kind of logic are rife in schools of education. For example, James P. Shaver argues that in a democratic, pluralistic society where value conflict is inevitable, each defendant's claim in a clash of values must be given equal consideration. To illustrate this interesting point of view, I quote from his survey on the scientific methods of value teaching entitled "Reflective Thinking, Values, and Social Studies Textbooks":

> In the dispute over racial segregation, the Negro's claims for integration are supported by our commitment to brotherhood, the equality of opportunity, and to equal protection of the law. By the same token, however, the segregationists' position has been defended in terms of freedom of association, of property rights, and even of the right to local control in such matters. Each of these is also an important American value.[18]

Yet to accuse the new teacher of this kind of relativistic thinking simply draws a shrug of the shoulders and a complacent reply: "You use one set of criteria for making value judgments; I use another. You fall back on traditional models and personal feelings. I examine past experience, related evidence, and all the possible consequences. Only then do I make up my mind. Yours is largely a conditioned reflex, mine a reasoned act. It's the only kind of response I accept as valid from my students."

"But isn't it possible," you argue, "just possible, for a value judgment to stand independent of the consequences—come hell or high water?"

"You mean the hang-tough values? What are they? Look, my friend, I use moral data in making judgment too. I love my parents, my wife, and my children. I am truly my brother's keeper. But this doesn't mean that I shouldn't put a value to the same kind of test as any other idea or judge its merits by the evidence."

13

"Can you always trust your evidence?" I ask. "Far more than my emotions," he replies. And so the conversation comes to a close.

This may be something of an exaggeration of the new teacher's philosophic outlook, but it is not entirely so. In comparing the educational practices of East and West, Clarence Faust, for one, has remarked on our increasing propensity to "refer questions of the truth of opinions and theories to the consequences of holding them, or at least to view propositions so attested as more substantial and valuable than those otherwise established."[19] Its implied methodology (that scientific methods are the way of all truth) is part and parcel of a great rash of inquiry-type programs in the social sciences now proliferating throughout America under the stimulus provided by Bruner, Fenton, and others. Surely, its flavor of pragmatist ethics, a là John Dewey and his distinquished colleagues, Sidney Hook, Abraham Edel, Max Otto, and others, is unmistakable. All is marked, in this calloused view of any distinction between an idea and a value, by irresolvable conflict between moral prescription and choice, and—what is perhaps its most pernicious feature—the Deweyan thesis that truth is operational, that effects rather than causes are its chief determinants.

Bertrand Russell, who agreed with John Dewey on most things, could not agree with him on this. The distinction he makes between his own view and Dewey's on this very critical point is most interesting. Russell considers a belief to be "true" when it has a particular kind of relationship to its causes. Dewey, on the other hand, gives what he calls "warranted assertability" to a belief only after assessing its effects or consequences. It is important to note, as Russell points out, that the past cannot be altered by present or future acts; therefore, if we assume that truth is the result of what has happened, it is completely independent of any influences that we may at present or in the future wish to exert upon it. But when truth or warranted assertability is gauged by future events, then, to the degree in which future events can be changed, it is also possible to change what should be asserted. Russell goes on to ask:

> Did Caesar cross the Rubicon? I should regard an affirmative answer as unalterably necessitated by a past event. Dr. Dewey would decide whether to say yes or no by an appraisal of future events, and there is no reason why these future events could not be arranged by human power so as to make a negative answer more satisfactory. If I find the belief that Caesar crossed the Rubicon very distasteful, I need not sit down in dull despair; I can, if I have enough skill and power, arrange a social environ-

ment in which the statement that he did not cross the Rubicon will have "warranted assertability."[20]

When embracing this view of what constitutes truth, how different becomes one's perspective on life! Shorn of the incubus of irrevokable human limitations, how enormously expanded is one's sense of freedom! Russell believed it was essentially this pragmatic outlook, so amenable to American industrialism and business enterprise, that gave to man the notion of unprecedented power he had no right to assume. In such "cosmic impiety" he sensed a danger that must ultimately lead to massive social dislocation and demise.

For my part, I have never questioned Dewey's lifelong devotion to humanitarian ideals nor his conviction that he had fashioned an ethic admirably suited to achieve them. I simply fail to see by what logic he closes the gap between means (the methods of science) and ends (moral synthesis)—a logic inescapably hinged on a fundamental contradiction: If you hold that the truth of a belief resides in the conditions that brought it into being, you will be apt to teach children that truth is more or less fixed and permanent, with intrinsic value; if you believe that truth is forged and tested in the marketplace, you cannot avoid giving it a shifting, opportunistic quality that men, even the most morally reflective, tend to manipulate for their own ends.

Although my purpose is far less cosmic in scope than Russell's or Dewey's, I nonetheless see in this linking of truth about values to the consequences of holding them a sinister influence upon value teaching no less deleterious in its effects. It is logical to assume, for example, that where consequences become the sole arbiters of truth, guiding principles begin to occupy a very uneasy position in the affairs of men. Such, in fact, is the very spirit that pervades the method called "valuing" (in contradistinction to value teaching). Simply stated, it is the method of assigning value to ideas and beliefs after an inquiry-type examination of them has proven them deserving of it. Touted as a scientific breakthrough in creating a responsible morality, it embraces most if not all of the techniques known to science: observing, comparing, summarizing, classifying, coding, criticizing, looking for assumptions, collecting and organizing data, hypothesizing, applying facts and principles, exploring alternatives, making decisions, designing projects, etc.

The list is indeed a mouthful, but there is far more involved. Under this formidable battery of techniques, all values of feeling and belief connected to some crucial issue are subjected to a pitiless spotlight of inquiry. No value that does not represent knowledge—that is to say, some proof of its own merits—is admissible. Values of pure feeling and emotion are suspect or soon become so for want of evidence. If, as some philosophers suggest, matters of true feeling fall outside the purview of science, so much the worse for feeling; everything is grist to the mill. A value such as compassion, for instance, in an investigation of adequate pensions for the elderly, would have a rough time of it, if indeed students had temerity enough to bring it into the discussion at all.

Within such an arena, then, scientific intellectualism provides the framework for decision making. Morality is seldom established; it is always being "discovered." Children are never set moral boundaries within which they may work out problems by whatever powers of mind have been vouchsafed them, but beyond which they may not venture. All is placed on the auction block, including the bargaining rules. Pitirim Sorokin, who is sometimes prone to be carried away by his own rhetoric, was not without justification when he said: "We live in an age in which no value, from God to private property, is universally accepted. There is no norm, from the Ten Commandments to contractual rules and those of etiquette, that is universally binding.... What one person or group affirms, another denies; what one pressure group extols, another vilifies.... Hence the mental, moral, religious, social, economic, and political anarchy that pervades our life and culture...."[21]

This conspicuous lack of any fixed signposts for the guidance of behavior is not without parallel in the classroom. During the Vietnam conflict, when Buddhist priests protested U.S. intervention by self-immolation, I watched senior students in a contemporary problems class formulate opinions, unchallenged by the teacher, that this kind of zeal was a species of fanaticism. The notion of such behavior as being essentially a moral problem, resolvable only in terms of moral absolutes, simply did not enter into the discussion. It could not; it would have been inundated by a mountain of intellectual considerations—political, economic, and social—that dominated the discussion. Later, when I asked the teacher (rather modestly, I thought) why this aspect of it had not been considered, he looked at me rather sharply.

"Isn't your approach a bit simplistic?" he asked. "We are dealing with a rather complex problem, you know."

"I suppose you're right," I replied, almost wishing I hadn't brought up the subject. "I thought, perhaps, it might have some relevance."

He relented somewhat. "You're talking about moral anchor points. Good Lord, man, have you been watching what goes on in Congress lately? That just isn't the way decisions are being made. I'm trying to prepare these kids for the real world."

I walked softly from the room, wondering if my whole intent

was not somehow grossly misdirected and naive.

Equally intriguing was my observation of a debating panel made up of bright seventh-graders who had been arbitrarily assigned the task of defending the position of the conscientious objector. It was obvious from the start that these students felt uncomfortable with their role, tending to equate pacifism with cowardice and disloyalty. It was also clear that no one had taken the trouble to point out to them that pacifism, in the tradition of the great Christian martyrs and of Gandhi, Martin Luther King, and others, can demand a courage as painful and difficult to maintain as that of a soldier on the battlefield. When, as generally happens in these cases, the whole argument was reduced to the ultimate test of the pacifist's belief—his severely limited choice of personal annihilation in preference to the destruction of another life—the entire concept was put down as somehow weird and irrational. The absence of any framework of real moral fiber had rendered this discussion a highly interesting though perfectly harmless intellectual exercise for both teacher and students.

Prescriptive morality is certainly a dubious virtue into which moral relativism often leads class discussion. During that same period of time there was a movement afoot to bring down into the primary grades the fruits of reflective thought. *Scholastic Magazine*, for example, which prints reading matter for millions of school children throughout America, was providing its huge readership with carefully researched and balanced arguments, pro and con, on the Vietnamese struggle. Some schools incorporated this material into their teaching of the Minnesota Plan, a major social science project of that period, whose professed "behavioral goals" included among others the learner who "respects the rights of others" and who "values human dignity."[22]

Such is the subtle nature of hypocrisy that few of us who practice it are aware that we are doing so. One elementary teacher I know, who could not equate the teaching of dignity for all humans with what was happening in Vietnam, collected pictures of Vietnamese children, all victims of the war. Lacerated and maimed, their flesh seared by napalm, they stared out from his bulletin board with tragic, pain-filled eyes. Class reaction was mixed; there was morbid curiosity, shock, and complaints of a "gruesome sense of humor." Nevertheless, every time the subject of Vietnam came up for discussion he admonished his class: "First, let's take a long hard look at those pictures, then we'll talk." As I watched I was strongly reminded of the tortuous search of Ivan Karamazov (from *The Brothers Karamazov)* for an answer to the evil of men's senseless cruelties. "But the children, Alyosha!" was the one question he kept hammering out again and again to his younger brother, who was training for the priesthood. "They haven't yet tasted of the apple. What about the children?"

It was to be expected that this young teacher, a rare gift to the profession, would be asked one day to answer the complaints of a parent who felt that his "political opinions" were dangerously prejudicial. On the second day he came before his principal; the third day his bulletin board was down; and on the fourth day he was again safely teaching reflective techniques.

Safely teaching, because the ideal teacher is one who never persuades, never weights the scale on any one side of a discussion, but rather guides his students to sources of information that will substantiate or refute their own beliefs. During this process of values clarification, the students, using all sorts of knowledge for testing their values, begin to slough off old and useless ideas, taboos, and other emotional hangups, gradually clearing the way for a new code of ethics characterized by flexibility, intellectual orientation, and a capacity for direct action.

Whatever reservations I may hold regarding the possibility of such an occurrence, this is not intended as a condemnation of values clarification, which has its own purpose and need. On the contrary, I consider it a matter of utmost importance for a person to discover if his values are those of a scoundrel, a saint, or a murderer.

The question of who is or who isn't a murderer, for example, deserves a moment's comment, since it bears distinctly on the new teacher's ability to use the "process of reasoning" in his own private judgments on important moral issues. Within the meaning of the term I would include a majority of the public at large. My feelings that this might be true were first formed in the early years of the Vietnam war, when any number of people I talked to assumed a strongly belligerent stance on policy questions about which they had only the foggiest notions. I was dismayed, but not without hope. There were still the teachers, in whose hands the prospects of a more humane world were safely ensconced. They were, after all, the largest and best educated teacher group in the world.

Alas, I had reckoned without checking my facts. As I entered into conversations with teachers, I found many of them amazingly truculent and warlike. It was a great disappointment to learn that, in spite of their sophisticated arguments, they were not different from the others. In vain did I try to point out how incompatible was our moral position with the facts of our own historical development—arguments that were being brilliantly and movingly advanced by Norman Cousins in the editorial pages of the *Saturday Review*. I had discovered a bitter truth: Teachers, like the rest of the people, are far more interested in exterminating their enemies than they are in the possibility of planetary extinction or of finding means of peaceful coexistence.

Even so, I should have been reluctant to take a public stand on this were it not for an incident that occurred several years later in which a large local branch of the National Education Association was asked to respond to the following resolution:

> Whereas the United States has been involved in Indochina for more than 20 years and whereas professional educators have a duty to voice their consciences concerning a terrible and unjust war, we ... call for an immediate withdrawal of all United States personnel from Indochina....

The resolution was turned down by a vote of five to two.[23]

Nowadays, of course, it has become fashionable to condemn the war on the ground that it was a gross blunder on the part of someone else. But the hypothesis that this new outlook reflects a fundamental change of heart is a notion upon which I look with the greatest suspicion.

The fact remains that most children come to the classroom with essentially humane attitudes. If such were not the case, this writing could have no purpose, for it has been rather conclusively documented by psychiatric researchers that the time from birth to age 5 or 6 is more crucial to attitude formation than all the years thereafter.[24] But for this average child, as Gordon Allport puts it, "the foundations of character were established by the age of 3 or 5, only in the sense that he is now *free to become*; he is not retarded; he is well launched on the course of continuous and unimpeded growth."[25] This would imply, of course, that the child's "natural" inclinations and dispositions toward behavior patterns which may be characterized as essentially humanitarian can be *selectively* reinforced and strengthened.

The same implication poses a question of grave import. What happens in an atmosphere in which primary attitudes and values are dealt with all of a piece, the trivial along with the significant, where choice is given free reign so long as it is based on consequential proof, where fixed guideposts and boundaries are either suspect or treated with no more reverence than yesterday's headline? This is certainly not to infer that moral prescriptions are mandates from heaven. For my part, I am willing to accept the social scientist's view—Ashley Montagu's, for one—that over great stretches of time a value system arises out of the most satisfactory relationship between human needs and environmental conditions and that to some degree this involves choice.[26] By the same token, choice without value, which severely restricts one's options, does not constitute morality; parading as such, it is opportunism, pure and simple. Choice takes on moral essence only when it transcends biology and acquires in doing so an arbitrary element that is at once inflexible and static in its demands. In rebuttal to Sydney Hook's contention that the source of one's sense of obligation or "ought" to others resides in the social pressures induced by other's needs and wants, Arthur Garnett (*The Moral Nature of Man*) states far more realistically, it seems to me, that one's "sense of obligation makes its demands quite independently of personal interest and social pressure and often directly counter to them. It demands loyalty to principles seen to be for the general human good, even...where such loyalty involves personal sacrifice."[27]

Surely, many moral judgments rise above Hook's criteria. Suppose a driver runs down a pedestrian on a lonely street in the dead of night. Although his first reaction is to escape, he stops his car immediately and attempts to render aid. Any amount of cerebration would inform him quickly of several ugly facts: He has been drinking, his driving record is bad, and if the pedestrian is seriously injured or dead he is apt to face a prison term.

Let us suppose further, that the pedestrian, a derelict on sight, is stone dead. Again the driver's impulse is to run, but instead he phones the authorities and waits submissively for their arrival. Why, in heaven's name? The victim is beyond all human assistance. True, facing up to his dilemma will do much to alleviate the driver's sense of guilt, but against this he must measure the moral obloquy and distress of possible imprisonment, the shame and financial hardship imposed on his family, and the probable ruin of his career. A rational examination of the consequences could reveal that guilt is by far the easier thing to live with.

Why, then, does he pick up the phone, deliberately choosing the more personally and socially disastrous of the two alternatives?

The facts seem to be that moral truth is often little concerned with consequences. Indeed, it would appear that many so-called moral judgments are not judgments at all, but more in the nature of compulsive behavior whose function it is to bring us up sharply when confronted with something our conscience tells us is deeply and morally wrong. In doing so it severely limits choice and often commits us to *total responsibility*.

Three

Truth and Logic

Science cannot prove that compassion is better than cruelty.[28]
—*Joseph Wood Krutch*

Apart from the rather dubious qualifications of most teachers to instill in the young a sense of commitment to commonly accepted principles, there is, in addition, a considerable problem in logic regarding their methodology. Whenever we act in accordance with some compelling belief that we accept as gospel truth, we do so on premises that involve two possible kinds of relationships. One is the relationship between the presumed truth of a belief and the criteria that establish its validity. The other is the relationship between truth and behavior. It is helpful to look at these one at a time, for they bear significantly on the nature of truth and its limitations in the decision-making process. Let us start out with the first relationship, that of truth to its criteria.

Since our concern is the inculcation of moral (or immoral) beliefs, it is important, first of all, to learn if there is anything essentially different between moral and intellectual truth or, put into another context, to find out what makes truth moral, as distinguished from any other kind of truth. We begin by pointing out what philosophers tell us about intellectual truth, since it is the kind most familiar to us. They use a number of ways—none completely satisfactory—for determining the truth or falsehood of a belief, but there is one that seems to be more acceptable than the others. It is simply that a belief is regarded as being true when it corresponds to an outside fact or group of facts placed in unique relationship to each other.[29] We might take the example of our belief in the truth of Ohm's Law. The example is purposely simple, but it serves us quite nicely. This law can be shown to be true just because the equation which tells that resistance is a function of current and voltage corresponds to experimental facts resulting from this relationship. Its truth rests upon the framework of this evidence, and whatever value it may have for us comes from our believing it and acting upon it.

It should be obvious, however, that many of our most revered moral beliefs can meet no such test. Our belief in God, in immortality, in compassion, in honesty—indeed, in truth itself—all are highly vulnerable to attack by any logician wishing to take an opposite view. There have been numerous attempts, of course, to demonstrate moral truth by the use of reason or the methods of science, but they are far from conclusive. When some forms of stealing are less of a gamble nowadays than, say, starting up a new business, it becomes increasingly difficult to prove that honesty is indeed the best policy (at least for the individual in the short term). All we can really say is that such beliefs are true only in the sense that they correspond to our feelings about them and perhaps to the degree in which they are universally held.

The fact that some beliefs are easy to prove while others are not has been further demonstrated in the work of the distinguished philosopher of logical analysis, Rudolph Carnap. A good example is the democratic ideal, *the right of equality*. Now, it must be admitted that whatever value we attach to this ideal, it will stem primarily from our feelings regarding it rather than from any demonstrated proof that all men do in fact have this right. In point of fact, in any kind of moral reasoning, as in the making of moral judgments or decisions, the one question that takes precedence over all others is the ultimate question of our feelings about what is good or evil—whether a thing is right or wrong, good or bad. But many statements such as the *right of equality*, as Carnap points out, are linguistic utterances having only an expressive function, not a representative one. They have no theoretical sense; they contain no knowledge; they can be proven neither true nor false.[30] This is obviously what Bertrand Russell meant when he talked about "things which are legitimately matters of feeling" whose investigations lie outside the province of scientific method.[31] As feeling states (intellectualized to be sure), they cannot be rationally tested, except in relationship to other feeling states, which suffer from the same limitations.

Our feelings, in short, are central to the issue. The condition is a slippery one for the proponent of scientific methods, for there is nothing in his repertoire of techniques that enables him to cope with this primary characteristic of value. Since he can only deal with data that can be proved or disproved, he must of necessity put all beliefs, either moral or intellectual, to the same test, without regard for the distinction that may greatly separate them.

The difficulties this problem raises are typified by the model on reflective techniques presented by Lawrence E. Metcalf. Through his books, co-authored by Maurice P. Hunt,[32] and his extensive survey of research in the field,[33] Metcalf has perhaps given us the clearest conception of Dewey's meaning of reflective thinking as it applies to the art of teaching.[34] Most important to this writing is his essentially pragmatic view of how teachers should deal with conflicting values that pervade so many public issues. To illustrate this view, I quote from one of his articles:

> Perhaps . . . a reinterpretation of problem solving . . . will help teachers to entertain the hypothesis that teaching people to be good is not their province. Teaching an understanding of how values affect and even distort perception is within their province. Teaching that certain values are inconsistent with other values is within their province as logicians. It is even their job to teach that some values are democratic.... But no one, least of all our teachers, can tell the American people what their values are to be.[35]

To demonstrate how this might work in practice, Metcalf sets up a classroom model in which students investigate the problem of socialized medicine. "If students are to decide whether they are in favor of socialized medicine, they will find it helpful to learn what socialized medicine is, and what results from it." During the learning process the teacher is encouraged to resist any temptation to "purvey" his own private biases. His job is to "help them find data, if it is available, on the achievements and other effects of socialized medicine" and to assist individuals in coping "with the logic of those who are opponents or proponents of this institution." He would have students speculate on what would be the effects of socialized medicine in this country and even ask them to rate these effects according to their "desirability" or "undesirability." By pursuing this method of nonintervention, teachers would no longer be teaching "values" but "valuing," by which Metcalf obviously means that ideas earn respectability or contempt by virtue of the evidence uncovered through reflective techniques.[36]

I do not argue with the general excellence of this approach. What I do object to is the implication that truly meaningful solutions to problems that involve conflicting values can be reached without reference to some *pre-established framework of commonly held moral reference points*. We are led to believe that reflective techniques alone will enable us not only to make the wiser of alternate decisions but to achieve a responsible moral climate.

But wherever conflicting values are present, especially strongly held ones, whose interpretation of what is wise behavior do we accept? As we have already noted, some of the most crucial issues are often most difficult to resolve on the basis of purely nonmoral data. Besides, it is no great trick for the clever protagonist to arm himself with a great mass of evidence in defense of any position he wishes to assume. Indeed, I watched the classic example of this truth a number of years ago when I chanced to see Edward Teller and Lord Bertrand Russell debate before a television audience the merits and shortcomings of nuclear armament. Seldom is one privileged to witness a display of such incisive rebuttal, pinpoint documentation, and prodigious range of knowledge. Yet even more fascinating than the brilliance of their arguments was the fact that both men, having spent lifetimes employing reflective techniques in the pursuit of new scientific knowledge, could arrive at positions so diametrically opposed. When men like these fall out over an issue embracing the fate of mankind, one is tempted to ask, somewhat cynically perhaps, if a bad decision is any less bad because it was made with full knowledge of the facts.

The need to teach reflective techniques is not in question here. Critical thinking should inform every proposed solution to the human predicament. But the solution itself must be the direct reflection of some fixed moral principle pinpointed somewhere on a scale of primary values. For example, if the value regarding human worth were truly operative—approaching, let us say, the intensity of Albert Schweitzer's concept of reverence for life—the idea of modern warfare as a solution to anything simply could not be countenanced. The immediate reaction to it would be one of such repugnance as to become virtually ego destroying. Reflective thinking might well be employed to examine alternate courses of action, but rarely if even one course of action is in direct conflict with the fundamental value itself.

If this sounds like some vastly artless oversimplification of a terribly complex problem, I should like to remind the reader that I am interested primarily in the elementary school child. A nodding acquaintance with the psychiatric view regarding the development of conscience, plus a number of years spent in personal observations, have convinced me that he is the main hope of the world. Thus it may not be within the province of teachers, as Metcalf suggests, to teach children how to be good, but we had better start telling them what social goodness means and what are some of its great motivating forces.

Finally, in addressing ourselves to the second relationship—that of truth to behavior—the proponent of inquiry must assume that children will automatically select what is demonstrably true over what is demonstrably false as a valid basis for his acts. In so doing he further contends that moral choice is really no different from acting upon conventional wisdom and that once we are taught the art of listening to the voice of "reason" our faculties of intellect will take charge of that part of man that still separates him from the angels: namely, his secret compulsions, his haunting dreams of power and position, his most deeply rooted psychological barriers to truth. Could former President Truman, if faced with incontestable proof, have brought himself to admit that his decision on Hiroshima was a terrible misjudgment? Would former President Johnson have bowed to overwhelming evidence of a tragic miscarriage of justice in Vietnam? Will former President Nixon ever make one move in the direction of admitting culpability and involvement in the Watergate scandals? I wonder. Powerful men with far greater perspicacity, whom history has proved wrong, have gone to their graves proclaiming the strategic accuracy of their decisions. Indeed, it would appear they could not do otherwise, for there must be some frightful immobilizing element in the act of losing face that is often self-destructive beyond limits that humans can endure.

Perhaps we may gain some insight into this strange condition by reviewing briefly the major theme running through the investigations of researchers such as Anna Freud, Rene Spitz, William Goldfarb, and others as compiled in John Bowlby's *Maternal Care and Mental Health.* Central to their findings is the lifelong and deeply pervading influence of attitudes internalized during early childhood—a phenomenon that Bowlby regards as the single most important psychiatric discovery in the past half century. Although his pronouncement is based on studies conducted with emotionally deprived infants and children, it is forcibly brought home to us that the principles are the same for everyone: a gradual accumulation of preferences, compulsions, and rejections eventually forms our life-style. As the first evidences of organized behavior, they precede the development of rational thought. Whether they are healthy or diseased is of no immediate concern; what does concern us is that, good or bad, they cast over our lives an invisible screen of primary dispositions and tendencies to behavior through which each of our thoughts is sifted and by which the very quality of our thinking is in large part determined.[37]

Such evidence of man's emotionally dominated rational processes has been even further advanced in the past decade by the work of ethologists such as Desmond Morris,[38] Konrad Lorenz,[39] and Robert Ardrey.[40] According to Morris, for instance, man emerged from the jungle onto the plains, a hunter, as aggressive and predatory as any animal on the scene. And so he remains, genetically unchanged to this day. While he preens himself on the technical know-how of a vastly superior mentality, it is the emotions surrounding the territorial imperative and the development of sexual equipment, unique within the primate kingdom, that continue to hold him in thrall and from which any real hope for release is pure fantasy.[41] So repugnant is this picture that many have spent the whole of their lives attempting to repudiate it. Yet the logic seems irrefutable. If, as Lorenz declares, man does indeed share with lower life the instinct of aggression, this must to some degree color his cognitive vision for so long as he remains in his present evolutionary state.

However, we need not even go this far. Any serious student of behavior, keenly aware of our likenesses as well as our differences, cannot fail to see that man's extreme difficulty in accepting "reason" outside the pale of his own dominant convictions and prejudices is a trait common to all of us. For example, two people with fundamentally different attitudes are able to agree on matters of only trifling importance. If they are colleagues of long standing and desirous of maintaining tolerable relations, they quickly map out the danger zones and skirt them cautiously, like two cats circling a bowl of hot porridge. More than likely, the one will view the other as something of a philistine or a fool, at least within these prescribed areas, and must often remind himself of the other's legal claim to voice opinions that seem to him disastrous. In such instances the injunction that he respect the opinions of his fellow man is too much to bear; it is enough that he grudgingly concede him the right to express them.

It is enlightening when lifelong proponents of "reason" with strongly differing viewpoints take up cudgels against each other. May I recommend to the reader, for an hour's entertainment, the exchange of letters between the late Bertrand Russell and John Fisher, the late senior editor of *Harper's* magazine, again on the subject of missile systems and thermonuclear warheads.[42] Russell's position against the bomb had been an embattled one for a number of years, of course, so we may perhaps forgive him for moments when his barbed witticisms got in the way of his arguments. But it really makes little difference. In spite of the mass of evidence in support of either position—indeed, because of it—one finds it impossible to come away with any nucleus of fact to give either side the clean edge of victory; the reader must simply take comfort in whatever he is most *disposed* to believe.

It ends, as such controversies usually do, in a cul-de-sac of exacerbated feelings and blunt, heavy-sided arguments colliding head-on. In all probability, neither man could have acquitted himself in any other way than he did. Inextricably bound in the mesh of his own style of viewing life, each had embarked on a course whose outcome was irreversible. As one psychologist concludes after a careful review of the experimental data, "Facts have relatively little impact on the man who has made up his mind.... It takes an overpowering array of facts to change the minds of people who are set in a belief that has emotional significance."[43]

It is for these very reasons that I see grave danger in a method of teaching that holds scientific intelligence as the chief arbiter of the decision-making process. Its implied dictum, *to follow wherever scientific intelligence may lead us,* may be the great hope of Alvin Toffler's *(Future Shock)* new era of super-industrialism; nevertheless, it is difficult to have lived more than 60 years without gaining some awareness of the cunning and rapacity of which men are capable in their determination to promote the good of mankind. Hence I tend to view civilization as a fragile veneer constantly in danger of being ripped away by the most logically conceived and carefully reasoned acts of violence.

Paradoxically, the sentiment expressed in the statement, "to follow wherever scientific intelligence may lead us," is typically identified with many men who combine great powers of thought with deep moral insight. When we examine the lives of such men, however, we often find a strange contradiction. Almost invariably their intellectual powers have been employed in the interests of promoting some profound moral outlook that suspiciously resembles an absolute. This assertion could be made of John Dewey no less than of Bertrand Russell. While such men would argue that action based on intelligence is better than action derived from simple moral conviction, they readily admit that unscrupulous men are often very intelligent. As leading advocates of scientific intelligence, they are in fact guilty of practicing what their formal systems of thought strongly disapprove: advancing arguments in terms of abiding moral principles. It is as if their most deeply rooted convictions had somehow escaped the steel trap of their own logic.

To the degree that schools bear some responsibility for perpetuating our democratic ideals, I see their major objective as one of combining children's need for a life of freedom with the amount of emotional conditioning that seems to me imperative to the maintenance of social stability and cohesion. I can think of no other way. Stability and cohesion, which strike me as key survival factors in any kind of society, can only be achieved by placing certain restrictions on the behavior of "autonomous man." While I sympathize with Edgar Friedenberg's repeated warnings about conformity as a major threat to his independence and freedom, I am also disturbed by his failure to deal with those human limitations which distinguish between autonomous behavior that is morally responsible as against that which is selfishly quibbling or anarchistic.[44] Such limitations, as I view them, are simply man's need to conform, from infancy onward, to certain personal and social mandates that in turn give him his private vision of what constitutes morally responsible behavior. Although private, it must correspond in large part to the views of his society. Bereft of this vision, the man is a psychopath. If the vision is too fragmented, he is the victim of every social wind, often chasing after ephemeral causes, incapable of attaining any goal that requires majority action. Whatever the case may be, at issue here is not that man conforms; rather, it is what he conforms to and how this process of conformity may be guided in such a way as to assure him a means of group survival while at the same time allowing him some life of the impulse. To achieve this end obviously calls for the reexamination of techniques that have traditionally remained within the shadow of what many educators describe as dangerous pedagogy.

Four

Do Teachers Have the Right To Indoctrinate?

You will also say, no doubt, that I am flirting with the idea of indoctrination. And my answer is again in the affirmative. Or, at least, I should say that the word does not frighten me. We may all rest assured that the younger generation in any society will be thoroughly imposed upon by its elders and by the culture into which it is born.... [45]

—*George S. Counts*

So spoke George Sylvester Counts, leading advocate of reformist education, to the convention of the Progressive Education Association in 1932. Stunned by the dangerous note of radicalism, PEA members were nevertheless moved to unprecedented heights of intellectual excitement and activity. Dare the schools build a new social order? Dare they abandon once and for all their comfortable role as keeper of outworn traditions and privilege? Dare they come to grips with widespread social inequality, the "glaring facts of industrialism," and the "emergence of a world society"? Only teachers themselves could spark this revolution, but in order to do so they must get rid of their timid notions about the "bogeys of *imposition* and *indoctrination* and teach the new vision with unstinting clarity and power."[46] Later, in recasting his speech for publication, Counts left no doubt of his meaning when he added that "all education contains a large element of imposition, that in the very nature of the case this is inevitable, that it is consequently eminently desirable, and that the frank acceptance of this fact by the educators is a major professional obligation."[47]

Reading these passages more than 40 years after they were written, one wonders if a majority of educators would buy any part of these notions today. It is difficult to say. There is no doubt many would, for reasons that range from honest philosophic belief to rigid doctrinaire attitudes. Others—among whose company I have met considerable numbers—would reject it out of hand, flatly denying it any place in the teaching act.*

---

*Counts himself had no second thoughts about indoctrination. Writing in response to an article I wrote for the December, 1969 *Phi Delta Kappan* ("Do Teachers Have the Right To Indoctrinate?"), Counts at age 80 told of a 1932 meeting at which he defended the thesis that a measure of indoctrination is inevitable. Dewey was present and remarked that he had checked the meaning of "indoctrination" in Webster's and discovered that it meant "teaching."

The fact remains that few principles in the teaching repertoire are more widely practiced or strongly reviled; widely practiced because in its least sophisticated form indoctrination constitutes far and away the easiest way to teach. The approach is either directly or indirectly authoritarian, a condition that eminently suits the natural dispositions of most human beings. The technique, moreover, eliminates for teachers the tiresome necessity of supplying alternatives.

Indoctrination is reviled for quite different reasons. It has been invariably judged inimical to democratic processes as they operate within the classroom. Examination of threats to academic freedom or freedom of choice, for instance, generally discloses some insidious form of imposition at work. It is most despised among older educators, I venture to say, for its association with the Nazi era in Germany. Ask any one of them what thoughts the term brings most vividly to mind and he will likely tell you about the inculcation of German youth with Nazi doctrine and all the evil it inspired.

Yet there is no gainsaying the power of the method. In less than a generation it fused an aimless, disoriented people into one smoothly mechanized social body. It replaced moral apathy with rancor and transformed a flawed national image into one of the most monstrous conceptions of racial superiority the civilized world has ever known. All in less than a generation.

In reviewing this astonishing feat, I for one cannot but stop to wonder: Need the method always lead to evil? Would it be justified were it able to help create the kind of world envisioned by Professor Counts? Was Counts right in believing that only through the presence of this "large element of imposition" could such a world spring into being?

Before attempting to answer these questions, it is important to reemphasize the fact that we are dealing with the inculcation of beliefs—dignity, human worth, the democratic freedoms, and the like—whose value in terms of intellectual truth is most difficult, if not impossible, to establish. Indeed, the more we think about it the more evident it becomes that such beliefs, if not valued for their own sake, are surely doomed to extinction. In this pragmatic world, so characterized by rapid change and the swift demise of institutions once believed impregnable, they simply will not stand the buffeting about by the consequences of holding them and survive. Because they cannot rely on scientifically defensible evidence and often lack empirical bases, they must be accepted on faith as absolutes or not at all.

Teaching children to accept truth on faith, however, calls for methods somewhat different from those for teaching them to accept truth on evidence. Absolutism does not lend itself fruitfully to argumentation or the employment of alternatives, for in a sense there are no acceptable alternatives to principles that are by definition "unconditioned, totally independent, perfect, and all-inclusive."[48]

This raises an interesting problem linked primarily to the teaching of literature. If Hemingway was correct in saying that one of the writer's greatest gifts is his sense of justice and injustice,[49] we may be sure that much of our best literature has been deliberately, if subtly, weighted on the side of virtue and the exposure of evil. Yet the condition is not always consistent with our most broadly accepted notions of what constitutes good teaching. Consider the position of the teacher. When a teacher presents all the alternatives with equal dedication and honesty, thus compelling his students to "make up their own minds," he follows what many critics consider the most desirable teaching pattern. Ideally, the situation calls for a careful disguising of all his own biases and the balancing out of every alternative for good or evil with one equally significant, or as nearly so as he can make it. In discussing *The Grapes of Wrath*, for example, he must in effect be prepared to say: "In his treatment of the dust-bowl farmer we see, on the one hand, Steinbeck's obvious commitment to brotherhood and human decency. Now this is all very well. But what about the claims of the fruit growers? The rights of property and economic gain are also important American values. Indeed, they have probably contributed more to our social well-being than all the rest put together."

Should the student ask the teacher for his own opinion on the relative importance of the values, the teacher must further reply: "Sorry, but I can't answer that. I have no right to establish a hierachy among values in terms of their priorities. That's your province. Besides, it wouldn't be good teaching. You see, I couldn't produce any real evidence to prove the superiority of one over the other, and I seriously doubt if anyone else could. Anything I said would have to be based on my own prejudices, which could be interpreted as indoctrination. I'm afraid the choices are yours and yours alone."

But Steinbeck was plainly not interested in the rights of the fruit growers. He was interested in "justice," and if, in the absence of an alternative novel dramatizing the fruit growers' claims, the teacher sticks closely to the novelist's own view, he is in serious trouble. Analysis may offer him some opportunity for presenting alternatives, but analysis is largely a tool for clarifying implication or inference, which is just another way the author has of telling us what he really thinks anyway. For surely an important test of dramatic literature is the skill with which it disposes of various alternatives in the interests of one or another, without violating our sense of probability. Unlike science, whose technique presupposes ignorance of truth, drama begins with a conceptual framework of truth logically inherent in its structure. Its strongest thrust, for this reason, is in the direction of absolutism, and the measure of drama's greatness is in no small degree the success it enjoys in achieving this condition.

Literature is amply supplied with such examples. In novel after novel we see the reenactment of this or that great truth or the plight of erring humans brought into conflict with the "fundamental" values for which there are no alternatives. What else is Norman Mailer's *The Naked and the Dead*, ultimately, but a statement of absolutism about the evil of war? As critic John Aldridge has said, "It is imperative to Mailer's purpose that the men of *The Naked and the Dead* be destroyed by the military ideology of war and that their destruction arise directly out of the action in which they are engaged."[50] Thus we see "Red" Valson slowly crushed by naked terror and the awful suffering of men whose minds and bodies are brutally punished through continuous combat. Lieutenant Hearn, once unafraid and detached, is broken by General Cummings, symbol of military fascism, and finally destroyed by the treacherous Sergeant Croft. Both the brilliant strategist, Cummings, and Croft, his enlisted counterpart, are nullified by ludicrous accidents, which are also a part of the best planned battles.

The interesting point is that nowhere in this powerfully sustained drama of nightmare and torment are there to be found alternatives that seriously challenge the author's central purpose. Mailer was not concerned, for example, with the possibility that the war *had* to be fought. His interest was in war per se and how it affected the human spirit.

Few writers were more enormously adept at stacking the deck against evil than Charles Dickens. To show us that we are instruments of benevolent impulses and a fundamental goodness that pervades all human nature was his overriding purpose. His techniques to prove this were an ebullient prose style, irrepressible imagination, and a sense of drama, sometimes powerful, sometimes verging on bathos. Nevertheless, in keeping with his aim, he succored the weak and the faint at heart, clothing his good people with bumbling kindliness, effervescent spirits, and the enduring patience to wait until something better "turns up." Against this portraiture of humble goodness he contrasted the Murdstones, the Heeps, and the Sikes, whose cunning and malevolence are drawn in grotesque lines, making them all the more loathsome to us.

Although Dickens primarily used the problem novel, we see in his work none of the intellectual sparring designed to give pause to our social and moral outlook that we find, for example, in the novels of Emile Zola. Dickens worked within no established philosophic framework, except perhaps his belief in the essential goodness of man. It is acknowledged that his erudition was slight, his logical faculties limited, and his literary taste somewhat confined. But no one's sense of justice and injustice had a surer touch than his. He probed the dark corners of society, dramatizing the evils of Chancery and the Yorkshire school system with a vividness that shocked the sensibilities of the English-speaking world. It is generally conceded that his books did more to alleviate the odious conditions they described than all the others of his day combined. If one novelist among thousands living and dead were chosen for his ability to inculcate man with the notion of his great potential for decency, Dickens would take his place head and shoulders above them all.

Even among important novelists whose moral themes are treated with far greater sophistication, we often find the same tendency toward absolutism. It is interesting that, when commissioned by the *Saturday Evening Post* to recommend for its readers a number of significant works of fiction, W. Somerset Maugham chose *War and Peace* in preference to *Anna Karenina* only after considerable deliberation. Although he later judged *Anna Karenina* as one of the world's outstanding novels, on this occasion he objected to it on the grounds that Tolstoy had had Anna deliberately killed because she violated the sanctity of the marriage vows. He complained of the novel as having "too much the aspect of a moral tract" and went on to say that because Tolstoy "strongly disapproved of Anna's love for Vronsky," it was imperative that he "bring it home to his readers that the wages of sin is death." There was no earthly reason, Maugham concludes, "except that Tolstoy had it in for her, why Anna should not have divorced her husband, whom she had never loved and who cared nothing for her, married Vronsky, and lived happily ever after."[51]

I am personally inclined to believe that Maugham was objecting less to Tolstoy's moralizing than to his choice of the moral. But of course Maugham was right; Tolstoy did have it in for Anna. He might have offered her some alternatives, as Maugham believed he should have, and still produced a great work. We shall never know. Tolstoy chose not to do so.

It is a matter of some significance that few important novelists, living or dead, have taken a serious view of pragmatist ethics. Even the occasional charge that Henry James gave in his novels the same relativistic treatment to values that his brother William James employed in the development of pragmatic philosophy[52] is open to serious question. The careful reader cannot fail to perceive that, as spokesmen for James's own social and moral judgments, the great majority of his literary protagonists carry about with them sets of values that are inflexible and diehard. This is not to say that he dismissed intelligence as a means of coping with life, or that he even relegated it to a secondary position. On the contrary, a singular treatment of intelligence, the Adamic Fall from innocence, was to be used over and over again in his novels and short stories. But if the fall, as James conceived it, implies anything, it is that intelligence most certainly cannot supply answers to all of life's problems and that it is at best subject to severe limitations. It became in his hands a unique instrument for showing us what happens when we run afoul of the moral code.

A typical example of this may be found in *The Portrait of a Lady,* considered by many as James's masterpiece. Isabel, a high-minded, lovely American girl, has been left a fortune that enables her to flit about the capitals of Europe imbibing knowledge and experience, for which she exhibits an uncommon thirst. Near the end of her itinerary she marries Osmond, a cruel and sinister egocentric whom she soon learns to despise. In having tasted of the fruit of knowledge, she has sloughed off many of her old standards and prejudices, so that the dissolution of an irksome tie should have been a relatively easy matter. But in the end, when Goodwood, a former admirer, begs her to escape with him to America, she refuses. In that moment of truth she realizes that she is not free; the limitations of tradition and convention have been thrust upon her, and her subsequent return to Osmond constitutes her awakening to the responsibility of a moral absolute.

It is true, of course, that not all great novels (*Madame Bovary,* for one) follow the pattern I have tried to describe. But surely enough of them do to warrant asking whether the teacher has any less right to tell it how he thinks it ought to be told than does the dramatist whose impact on moral attitudes is perhaps next only to that of the home. Does he have the same privilege of deliberately weighting the scale in matters to which science or reason can supply but few legitimate answers? Does he have the same right to inculcate youth with the notions of trust, fidelity, and compassion when he knows that fully half the world he lives in is still brutalized by violent struggles for identity and survival?

There is no denying, of course, the evil ends the concept of imposition has been put to or the vast danger involved in its use. In the hands of the Germans it built national purpose through a hatred generated by dramatizing and exaggerating abuses, both imaginary and real, since World War I. Yet the method, when brought under the influence of identification (and I seriously question its effectiveness under any other condition), is closely allied to the spirit of drama. Within this setting it depends for its success not on presenting alternatives in terms of facts and concepts, but upon the skills of emotional suasion and empathy; on metaphor and characterization; on narrative, conflict, and resolution. The backdrop to all this is absolutism and the deep and willing suspension of judgment to the perfect, all-encompassing principle: one belief, one choice, one view of life, one way of behavior, selected in a moment of time against all others, because it provided within each of us a powerful wish-fulfilling function. It may even bear some resemblance to Skinner's definition of operant behavior, in which a *prearranged environment selects* the right behavior for reinforcement, thus increasing the chances of forming certain habits that tend to be perpetuated and working toward the benefit of the individual and the group. If it is in one sense a blind act on the part of the learner; it is also a subtle re-creation of experience, a way of forging, changing, or solidifying attitudes through fantasy and subliminal suggestion. Put to one purpose, we call it propaganda; put to another it comes out a story or a play espousing noble causes. But call it what you will, the tools are precisely those found in the dramatist's stock-in-trade.

It is necessary to point out here that I have no argument with the employment of alternatives as a means of teaching what is, or passes for, learned opinion. Indoctrination under these conditions would be intolerable, and the teacher is wise who stands guard against this insidious form of inculcation. A hundred years ago Charles W. Eliot made a statement regarding this matter; it remains the classic answer. "Philosophical subjects," he said, "should never be taught with authority. They are not established sciences; they are full of disputed matters, open questions, and bottomless speculations. It is not the function of the teacher to settle philosophical and political controversies for the pupil, or even recommend to him any one set of opinions as better than another. Exposition, not imposition of opinions, is the professor's part. The student should be made acquainted with all sides of these controversies...."[53]

But Eliot spoke primarily of intellectualization, not of identification through which the internalizing of attitudes and values occurs. While it is true that intellectualizing consciously held attitudes helps to strengthen them considerably,[54] the evidence breaks down when other factors enter upon the scene. Studies have shown, for instance, that attitudes with strong emotional counterparts are virtually impregnable to informational approaches.[55] In unstructured situations, moreover, where nonexis-

35

tent or latent attitudes may be brought to fruition, it is important (if you wish to form a particular attitude) to "draw conclusions" for learners rather than to leave them suspended between the horns of a dilemma.[56] How we approach the teaching act, obviously, depends on our intent.

There is, in addition, the simple fact that the employment of alternatives within certain contexts is an anachronistic pursuit, except perhaps as an occasional means of providing historical insight or re-creating the moral and spiritual conflict of the race—a more important task. Any attempt to present all the alternatives to equality as a human ideal, for example, would necessitate making a viable case for slavery. The notion is not as ridiculous as it sounds. If history has had anything to say, the idea of equality as a universal concept is sheer nonsense. For skeptics regarding early American attitudes, I heartily recommend the reading, "Hugh Jones on the Benefits of Slavery to the Negro," found in Max Savelle's *The Colonial Origins of American Thought.*[57] The Greeks, as we know, lived comfortably with slavery, accepting it as a perfectly normal condition of their lives. One of the most incredible ironies to come from that period, or from any other for that matter, was that the leisure allowed by the practice of slavery enabled the Greeks to invent democracy, its archenemy. Except for sporadic rebellions fictionalized in such accounts as *Spartacus* and *The Confessions of Nat Turner,* the absolute power of life and death exercised by one human over another has been the fact of our race throughout all but a tiny portion of its long and troubled history. There was, to be sure, a growing disenchantment with slavery, but up until a century ago it persisted as a highly successful human innovation. So long as the slave was someone who you happened not to be, it was easy enough to find perfectly acceptable reasons—social, moral, or biological—for continuing the practice of slavery.

Although all the evidence, the real evidence by which imposition or indoctrination must be judged, is not in, what there is of it seems to point to a single inescapable fact: The principle is singularly and irrevocably linked to the process of internalizing attitudes. To be more specific, identification becomes *selective* only when teachers bias their arguments in favor of those values society wishes to perpetuate. Some psychologists bluntly define the school's unique role in this matter. Lee J. Cronbach, in particular, believes that "The teacher...has an obligation to intensify his influence by whatever procedures will have the greatest effect.... One must remember that, if, on first thought, we...object to the suggestion that teachers engage in propaganda, part of the teacher's duty is to communicate the ideals of the culture."[58] Thus we may sympathize with harassed principals who admonish their teachers: "If we're to be stuck with teaching sex education to pupils, for God's sake don't make the mistake of imposing your own values onto the student." Yet, as the evidence seems to show, it is precisely in the act of imposition that specific attitudes begin to form.

The statement, in point of fact, reflects one of our most serious problems in this area of teaching. With so much ambiguity and conflict in our society at large, determining what values to teach, let alone how to go about teaching them, is always a nagging concern, and sometimes a very threatening one. Because agreement on such questions is almost impossible to reach, it is little wonder that some critics voice grave reservations about the schools' involvement in this kind of pedagogy.

Social scientists, who are now reportedly spending more and more of their time in search of universal man, may be able to provide some answers. The late anthropologist Ralph Linton announced not long before his death that this was the most significant task to which the social scientist could dedicate his life and his work.[59] It is my impression that his work will turn up little of importance that men of letters have not known intuitively for centuries. Still, the leap from intuitive knowledge to practical application is a painful one and often impossible to make without the aid of scientific midwives who first "check the information" before giving us the green light. Whatever their consensus may be, I would sooner stake my bets (and my best hopes) on 10 children reading *Uncle Tom's Cabin* under the auspices of a sensitive teacher dedicated to Harriet Beecher Stowe's message than upon 100 adults pursuing a scholarly examination of Mills's treatise, *On Liberty.*

Five

The Limits of Social Education

Newborn babies were little computers waiting to be pro-
grammed, and they would learn whatever they were taught,
from bad grammar to bad attitudes. Like computers, they were
undiscriminating; they had no way of discriminating between
good ideas and bad ones. The analogy was quite exact; many
people had remarked on the childishness and literalness of com-
puters. For example, if you could instruct a computer to "Put
on your shoes and socks," the computer would certainly reply
that socks could not be fitted over shoes.

All the important programming was finished by the age of 7.
Racial attitudes, sexual attitudes, ethical attitudes, religious at-
titudes, national attitudes. The gyroscope was set, and the
children let loose to spin off on their predetermined courses.[60]
—Michael Crighton

While I may have left readers with the impression that changes
in student behavior may be rather easily affected by the employment of techniques traditionally considered "dangerous pedagogy," I now find it necessary to pause—even to back up somewhat—and point out that, whatever techniques may be used,
the difficulties hampering schools in their implicitly assigned
role of socializing America's children into the democratic mold
are enormous and complicated. When experts tell us with increasing urgency that within the critical period between birth
and ages 5 and 6 lies the key to almost all that will follow in the
child's social and emotional development, that such development, moreover, is for reasons we shall explore largely irreversible, and that it is significantly tied to cognitive functioning—then one can only infer that there are no truly meaningful
approaches to the problems besetting education today unless
educators are given a new mandate by the people that provides
for some real control over the first six years of the child's life.

Indeed, it would appear from a growing body of evidence that,
contrary to highly romanticized indictments of the school's
failure to meet its social and academic responsibilities, *preschool*
children in larger and larger numbers are no longer programmed

to succeed. This distinct possibility, which brings into painful focus the beleaguered school's impotence in the face of modern realities, is strongly reflected in the social scientist's growing concern over America's children as revealed in the following excerpts from the White House Conference on Children held in 1970:

> America's families, and their children, are in trouble, trouble so deep and pervasive as to threaten the future of our nation. The source of the trouble is nothing less than a national neglect of children and those primarily engaged in their care—America's parents....[61]

Such critical remarks, supported by the heavily documented evidence found in the conference, constitute, in the words of national chairman Stephen Hess,

> ...a broad commentary on America—and a deeply disturbing one. They indict America for vast neglect of its children. They challenge the proposition that ours is a child-centered society. Instead they say that the child—as far as our institutions and laws are concerned—is too often a forgotten American.[62]

There is more recent evidence of this condition which we shall examine in the following pages. Meanwhile, Hess goes on to say that in our country today the life-style is such that "children and families come last." American society, furthermore, "whether viewed in comparison to other nations or to itself over time, is according progressively less attention to its children," a pattern that begins to emerge from the moment the child is born.[63]

Nor have older children escaped the encroaching incubus. Anticipating the accounts of the White House Conference on Children by 10 years, James S. Coleman, in describing the world of the teenager of the early Sixties, already foresaw that adolescents were being "cut off, probably more than ever before, from adult society." True, they were still "oriented toward fulfilling their parents' desires," but now they were also beginning to "look very much to their peers for approval.... " As a consequence, "our society has within its midst a set of small teen-age societies, which focus teen-age interests and attitudes on things far removed from adult responsibilities, and which may develop standards that lead away from those goals established by a larger society."[64]

It is doubtful that even Coleman, with an ear so keenly attuned to the changing behavior patterns in youth, could have dreamed of the degree of alienation from adult standards the next 10 years would bring, or how dramatically this alienation would be reflected by the soaring rates of juvenile drug abuse, delinquency, violence, and crime marked by increased savagery—again, all carefully documented by the White House Conference. According to these data,

> ... the proportion of youngsters between the ages of 10 and 18
> arrested for drug abuse doubled between 1964 and 1968; since
> 1963 juvenile deliquency has been increasing at a faster rate
> than the breaking and entry (sexual assault and murder are now
> statistically significant additions to the list); and, if the present
> trends continue, one out of every nine youngsters will appear in
> juvenile court before age 18. These figures index only detected
> and prosecuted offenses. How high must they run before we
> acknowledge that they reflect deep and pervasive problems in
> the treatment of children and youth in our society?[65]

While such accounts of crime among youth are now commonly
accepted truth, less well known are its fundamental causes and
the debilitating effects they have had, and continue to have, on
the school's ability to induce important changes in the attitudes
of children, either academically, socially, or morally. Like
submerged portions of icebergs, the real obstacles facing schools
are gargantuan, stemming primarily from three sources: first, our
historically developed political-economic system; second, what I
shall call (for want of a better term) biological determinism; and
third, the impact of a technology that is perhaps the most highly
developed and sophisticated in the world. All three must be
understood as distinct problems if we are finally to bring to the
schools' dilemma solutions that take a step beyond the romantic
and often incredible diatribe of such writers as John Holt, Ivan
Illich, and Paul Goodman, or the interesting and clever
palliatives offered by Robert Glasser, or Neil Postman and
Charles Weingartner.

We begin with a brief review of some peculiarities found in our
historically developed political-economic system and try to determine how they have influenced education in America for better or
for worse. Most recognized historians of education (Freeman
Butts and Lawrence Cremin, for instance) tend, perhaps un-
consciously and not without good cause, to present our developing school system as a unifying force—an instrument ingeniously
adapted to meet the needs of a society which, from its very inception, has been caught up in steady and often tumultuous social
and economic change. Granting the importance of this message,
I should like to point out a factor, frequently underplayed or
overlooked, that is inherent in our way of life: namely, the lingering and pervasive ambivalence with which American society has
regarded, and continues to regard, the school in terms of its purposes, its worth, its effectiveness, and, as a direct reflection of
these, the degree of public willingness to support any universal
concept of equal educational opportunity.

Such ambivalence can in large part be traced to the origins of
the American educational system and to the simple fact that,

both by accident and by choice, we happen to be living within a uniquely developed form of democratic government. For an account of this somewhat unusual period, Professor Max Savelle, a prominent authority on colonial history and its impact on American life and thought, offers some helpful insights. Although education in the colonial settlements, he tells us, shared the primary goal of "transferring English culture across the generations," there were considerable differences among the colonies in *what* was to be transferred and *how* it was to be accomplished. For early education was the offspring of three fairly distinct sociological groups. One of these was the Anglican group, a society with strong aristocratic leanings, which composed the southern colonies and those of the British islands of the Caribbean. Its English gentry attitude, aimed at producing the cultivated gentleman, together with the rise of the sparsely distributed plantation system, led to a strong belief that education was strictly a personal affair, a kind of "private enterprise, conducted by tutors or small private schools."[66] A typical sentiment of the time was expressed by Governor Sir William Berkely of Virginia in reply to the question of how the children were taught:

> The same course that is taken in England out[side] of towns; every man according to his ability instructing his children.... But, I thank God, there are no free schools nor printing [in Virginia], and I hope we shall not have these hundred years; for learning has brought disobedience, and heresy, and sects into the world, and printing has divulged them, and libels against the best government. God keep us from both![67]

This is of course the epitome of conservatism, reminiscent of a day and age, one fervently hopes, that will never return. Nevertheless, its echoes, though muted and cleverly disguised, still frequently reverberate through the halls of Congress.

We turn with pride to the second and third sociological groups, the Puritan dissenters who founded the New England colonies, and the subdivision of these, the Quaker pietists (with German intrusions) who established settlements in New York, New Jersey, and Pennsylvania, later known as the Middle Colonies. With this common British ancestry, one would think that ideas about the significance of education would reflect considerable agreement among the populace. To a degree this was true. Along with the general belief that "knowledge and the trained mind were closer to the virtuous life" (and to the fulfillment of democratic ideals, as Jefferson was to say later) came the first glimmering of the concept of universal education, based, curiously enough, on the Protestant belief that, because salvation was individually attainable through a correct interpretation of the Bible, minimal reading skill was mandatory for every child. Thus we witness the first educational laws of 1642 and 1647 in which the colony of Massachusetts required every town of 50 or more families not only to provide schools but also to support them with tax monies.[68]

But even in so noble an experiment there was little unanimity in how education should be implemented or what were to be its outcomes. As Savelle points out, it was not long before large Anglican segments began sharing the gentlemanly educational ideals of their neighbors to the south.[69] In keeping with this aristocratic temperament, Jefferson's proposal, years later, of a two-track system of education, one for leaders and one for the common man, could not but help promote an elitist educational philosophy, prevalent to this day, in spite of his yeoman work for the public support of schools.

Contrary to this view, the Quaker pietists regarded education not only in the light of its religious significance but also—and primarily—as a means of preparing youth for useful occupations. It was Benjamin Franklin who became the ultimate spokesman for this position, conceiving of education as a flexible, pragmatic instrument designed to resolve problems of a burgeoning society soon to be plagued by language barriers, an emerging science, and an expanding frontier with emphasis on adaptability and innovation.[70]

As a consequence, we have inherited, on the one hand, an eclectic, private vision of educational excellence, based in no small part on the premise that equal opportunity for all can only lead to a leveling process equivalent to mediocrity and, on the other, a public view that excellence is to be measured by the people's guarantee of strict parity in the quality and amount of exposure for every American child.

Although, as a democracy, we are committed to the latter position, our country, from its very inception, has regarded education as a negotiable item. Historians are well aware of the enormous difficulties that threatened ratification of the American Constitution. Prior to that historic event, we are told, the 13 colonies "had become so disorderly that men spoke of possible war between them."[71] Suspicions, dissentions, and anarchy, touched off by broken agreements, prostrated markets, land foreclosures, the proliferation of worthless paper money, inordinately heavy tax burdens without public sanction—these were but a few of the problems dividing the people and the colonies. Some key questions being asked: Would not a strong central government lead to insidious forms of tyranny? What about tax oppression? Wouldn't the states be dragged into costly foreign wars?[72]

As we read the account of this crucial period, it is impossible to escape the notion that one fundamental thread of fear runs through all the highly volatile and desperate negotiations: the awesome threat to personal property—however indirect, whatever its form. This should come as no surprise; the august body composing the ratification committee was, after all, made up of prominent business leaders, large plantation owners, and men in highly skilled professions. One can only speculate, of course, but as a prolific educational writer and dedicated proponent of the virtues of universal education, for example, Ben Franklin could not have failed to recognize the extremely important relationship between a thriving democracy and an educated electorate. As a shrewd economist and businessman keenly aware of how cunningly matters of profit and loss shape one's judgments, he also knew, as did the others, that any impending tax burdens that could be judiciously left to state control would present no immediate threat to ratification, the overriding objective of the convention. As if by tacit consent, education was not even listed on the roll of items considered imperative to the proper functioning of our nation.

Unfortunately, as history has shown us, leaving the future of education to the predilections of each state was often tantamount to abdicating responsibility for both its quality and its existence as an institution. Over the years a patchwork of legislation intended to correct this original lack of commitment has emanated from Washington, some generous and far-seeing, some niggardly and myopic; nevertheless, the pervasive sense of ambivalence still remains.

Perhaps, in the final analysis, it resides most fundamentally in our peculiarly oriented political structure. Professor Savelle points out that in an open society such as ours criticism from conservative quarters as well as from the liberal side must be accepted as a part of the normal democratic process, no matter what the issue at stake. He makes no reference, of course, to the enormous difficulties inherent in the process—which is not to imply that parents should be denied the right to decide what schools should teach their children, but simply that the condition offers little assurance that any teaching will take place at all. This fact was brought dramatically into focus by a frustrated Ohio citizen in the wake of that state's 1977 school funding crisis. "Federal money," he bitterly complained, "is readily voted for new armament, military research, multi-billion-dollar space projects, foreign aid to corrupt governments, even for subsidies to tobacco companies indirectly responsible for the highest known incidence of lung cancer on earth. But for an institution which for over 200 years has stood guardian over the very ideals that have helped insure this nation's freedoms and general well being, there is no money."[73]

But even granting that schools, by some miracle, will be assigned new responsibilities for the guidance of children's early unfolding years, we would still have no guarantee that educators will quite know what to do with them. Yet, if we may believe the evidence that researchers have uncovered only within the past few decades, the significance of this period in terms of behaviors that will color and dominate the child's whole future is nothing less than startling.

Conventional knowledge that speaks of childhood as the most formative years ("as the twig is bent, so the tree's inclined," etc.) tells us only half the truth and then by no means the most important half. It is, in the words of leading ethologists such as Konrad Lorenz, Eckhard Hess, Desmond Morris, and others, an extraordinarily sensitive period in the development of the organism (animal or human) when a small amount of experience will produce a powerful and enduring effect on later life.[74] From Hess's comprehensive survey of the research literature we learn that such effects

> ...are regarded as being due to special characteristics of the young animal or infant. These special characteristics do not arise from its being a relatively inexperienced organism but from its particular developmental condition—that is, its biological situation. A young organism differs from the not so young not only in the amount of experience but also in neurological and physiological structure and functioning. This means that its susceptibility to different types of experience can differ radically from the susceptibility of an older organism to the same experiences. It can be more sensitive to certain types of events and less sensitive to other classes of events because of *biological,* not just experiential, differences.[75]

The phenomenon, which is called imprinting, was first brought to the attention of the scientific world through the animal studies of Konrad Lorenz, who ascribes to the condition a genetically designed purpose whereby certain "innate releasing mechanisms (IRMs) roughly represent a 'keyboard' by means of which the environment plays on the 'organ of drives.... ' " These IRMs or "templates," at specific stages in development, assume a high state of readiness, so that "if a perceptual object or a process in the environment fits such a template the corresponding drive activity will be released."[76]

Although the period of susceptibility among some animals may spread out over a length of time, for others it is often of critically short duration, depending on the inherited characteristics of the species to which it belongs. The Canadian psychologist D. O. Hebb, of McGill University, for example, tells us that rats complete all their visual learning in a matter of 15 minutes, while primates may require several weeks or months to achieve the same thing.[77] The critical socialization period for a puppy, according to John Scott and J. P. Fuller, is one in which, surprisingly, very brief exposure to perceptual objects, either animal or human or both, shortly after three weeks of age, will create powerful social bonds "which can be duplicated only by hours or weeks of patient effort at later periods in life—*if, indeed, it can be duplicated at all.*" Of such "great change and sensitivity" is this period, moreover, that it virtually determines "which animals and human beings will become his closest social relatives...all the rest of his life."[78]

Because for many animals, Lorenz explains, these are "instinctive acts, performed only once in a lifetime...the animal has to 'get it right' the very first time," meaning of course that the correct response must be matched up with correct external stimuli.

For this reason, too, "the survival of the species and of the individual is guaranteed only because these internal dynamics are adjusted to external situations which occur with a certain regularity."[79]

I have quoted briefly from these animal studies because they explain more clearly and forcefully the "classic" condition that occurs in imprinting, and also because an increasing number of social scientists are beginning to note strong parallels to imprinting in human development. Of particular interest to them is the question of what happens when such "external situations" *do not* occur with a "certain regularity," or if in some bizarre and unprecedented way they become distorted by environmental influence, or if there is misalignment with the "internal dynamics" of the organism. A typical case of misalignment, familiar to most of us, centers around the difficulties of acquiring a new language. Repeating from Hess the premise that certain learning processes are automatic during what ethologists call "optimal" periods of readiness, he states that normally somewhere near the age of 3 a "child picks up the structure of his mother's tongue—*without being taught*—and from then on to the age of 6, a tremendous vocabulary development takes place, one which adults rarely duplicate."[80] However, if the external situation is somehow not in harmony with the organism's state of readiness, or if readiness has already expired, learning will invariably become stunted.[81] It is a generally accepted fact, for example, that after the age of 9 or 10 the ability to learn a new language with ease diminishes rapidly, so that, except in rare instances, great precision in thought and pronunciation become virtually impossible to achieve.[82]

An even more significant extension of this phenomenon comes from the research of Glen Dolman, Robert Dolman, and Carl Delacato, who investigated what appeared to be neurological impairment in reading, speech, and related disabilities. If one were asked to diagnose the cause of a particular speech problem, for example, the standard response would likely derive from either Freudian or behaviorist psychologies—a malfunctioning superego, perhaps, or bad conditioning practices. What we learn instead is

> ...the amazing fact that certain physical activities are apparently essential for proper neurological functioning involved in intellectual processes. One of the most important of these physical activities is the baby's cross-pattern crawling, which normally occurs from the age of 6 months to 12 or 14 months. The function of crawling, in addition to locomotion, is to develop the synergistic action of the two halves of the brain. If this neurological development fails to occur because of child-rearing practices which inhibit crawling experiences, then the child may appear to be mentally deficient or, in borderline cases, to have reading and speech difficulties. The same basic problem—incompleteness of neurological organization—is reflected in a whole continuum, ranging from aphasia, delayed speech, stuttering, retarded reading, poor spelling and handwriting, to reading which falls within normal range but is below mathematical performance.[83]

Again, we may safely predict that corrective measures would surely involve an intensive program in various *skill-oriented* sensory and motor training techniques—remedial techniques that are presumed to be directly related to the nature of the disability. But instead of repeated exercises in visual and sound discrimination, we are told that therapy in which "the child is made to perform the cross-pattern crawling has produced spectacular improvement in these areas of intellectual functioning."[84]

This does not mean, of course, that all learning disabilities stem from the child's thwarted efforts to crawl, or that Freud or Skinner would be dead wrong in their assessment, let us say, of a child's speech problem. It is obvious, however, that here we are dealing with a whole new concept of how a great deal of the child's most important learning occurs—a concept to which educators have had little if any exposure, and over which they exercise absolutely no control. What they have been exposed to, for certain, are numerous association learning theories, of which behaviorism is perhaps most typical. The difference, Hess insists, is one of great significance:

> There are important consequences of the fact that the imprinting object is from the outset an unconditional stimulus (food) rather than a neutral one (Pavlov's bell, for example) which acquires a certain meaning for the animal. In classical conditioning, as a rule the conditioned stimulus will gradually lose this meaning when it is no longer associated with the unconditional stimulus. This process is called extinction.... In social and food imprinting, however, the object itself is an unconditional stimulus, which means that the question of extinc-

tion does not enter in the same degree or the same fashion. In fact, in normal conditions it may not enter at all. In studies of learning in very young organisms, it has been found that occasional repetition of the learning is necessary to prevent forgetting. However, this does not occur in cases where social imprinting has been involved: the imprinting object is not forgotten when there is prolonged absence. In addition, the imprinted object is its own reinforcer....[85]

In his extensive work with the autistic child, Bruno Bettelheim of the University of Chicago borrows heavily from the research of the ethologists, noting strong similarities to imprinting in the child's development, especially when the imprinting process has malfunctioned in one way or another. As a neo-Freudian, following closely in the footsteps of John Bowlby, Rene Spitz, and Anna Freud, he is expressly concerned with the relationship between emotional experience and cognitive functioning, which he views as being critically dependent on a "biological time clock" or an "inborn time schedule that cannot be delayed for too long."[86] Numerous clinical investigations have convinced him that, while there may be no clearly defined time schedule for the "development of the emotions, there is one for *the intellectual development—based on those emotions.*" In a sense, timing for humans is more a relative concept than an absolute one; nevertheless, it is crucial. "If the requisite emotional experiences," he points out, "are not available to the child before puberty sets in— that is, at the time when it is necessary for the unfolding of his full intellectual (or ego) development, then the ego remains stunted...."[87]

Bettelheim describes two critical periods of sensitivity that, prior to the onset of puberty, closely duplicate those outlined by Hess and his colleagues. The first of these begins at about six months of age, when visual discrimination becomes well enough established to differentiate between persons and objects that are familiar as opposed to those that are foreign or strange. It is often a period of extreme polarization when unfamiliarity is equated with fear or unfriendliness, a situation that often gives distress to friends and neighbors whose overtures are invariably rejected as the infant quickly turns and buries his face in the mother's breast. In contrast to his previously generalized smiling and crooning, this behavior has been variously described as one of the first significant socialized responses to a single object, resembling to some degree the following behavior observed in lower animals and carrying with it the same implications of genetic programming for survival.[88]

Only during the second critical period of development—starting at about 18 months of age—when "language and locomotion turn the infant into a child," does his few positive reactions begin to include members outside his immediate household. For the first time now, the child is able to exercise control over his environment with a degree of mastery. Indeed, it is like the three-weeks-old puppy off on his first social investigations.

> ...the human infant can now, through walking and talking, "approach or avoid another individual." He can toilet-train himself, as opposed to being trained against his wishes. And again, what happens in this second sensitive period builds to a very large degree on what happened before; on what view of the world he has so far developed and into which he must now fit newer experience.[89]

When Bettelheim speaks of the effects of "what happened before" and the child's "view of the world," he is most certainly referring to the first of Erik Erikson's now classic "Eight Ages of Man," a theoretical foundation of child development to which so many psychologists owe much of what is contained in their own child development theories. Erikson's first "age," entitled *Basic Trust Versus Basic Mistrust,* is strongly predicated on the ethologist's view of sensitive periods, but with greater emphasis on the socializing process, which begins almost at birth. And for good reason. It is hard, for example, to deny Shakespeare's assessment of the new-born child who enters the world "an infant, mewling and puking in the nurse's arms," with very little to recommend him at this stage of life or in the weeks that immediately follow. Only by the most deliberate exercise of our romantic sensibilities could we attribute to this behavior any of the virtues that set him apart as a human. And yet, if we can accept Erikson's appraisal of this phase of his development, it is, in a social sense, the most crucial one he will ever pass through. For upon the quality of his oral and other physical experiences will be established his fundamental trust or mistrust of the world—a factor, Erikson goes on to say, that in no small part determines not only the success of his future interpersonal relationships but the kinds of values he will choose to live by.[90]

Erikson's analysis of this socializing process strikes me as most admirable, both in terms of profound clinical insight and the power of logic. Social trust in the baby, he explains, is gradually internalized through:

> ...the ease of his feeding, the depth of his sleep, the relaxation of his bowels.... In his gradually increasing waking hours he finds that more and more adventures of the senses arouse a feeling of familiarity, of having coincided with a feeling of inner goodness.... The infant's first social achievement, then, is his willingness to let his mother out of sight without undue anxiety or rage, because she has become an inner certainty as well as an

outer predictability. Such consistency, continuity, and sameness of experience provide a rudimentary sense of ego identity which depends, I think, on the recognition that there is an inner population of remembered and anticipated sensations and images which are firmly correlated with the outer population of familiar and predictable things and people. [91]

Closely related to the dynamics described by Erikson is the Freudian principle of *identification*, which we have briefly introduced in a previous chapter. Because of its potential as a concept of special significance to teachers, it seems appropriate, before dealing with its applications, to describe identification more clearly in terms of its nature and purpose.

Theorists are not entirely agreed on the time when identification as a process for internalizing behaviors first begins to assume an active role. Erikson sets it at about six months, when "mutuality" or the mutually fulfilling behaviors that characterize sensitive maternal care begin to take on meaning for the child. [92] As a psychologist of cognitive processes, Piaget thinks it occurs at about 18 months, by which time intellectual development has become sufficiently advanced. [93] Stanford psychologist Robert Sears believes identification most clearly establishes itself as an identifiable principle at about age 3, although he concedes that Erikson may be correct in tracing its roots to the quality of the mother/child relationship during infancy. [94]

On several things they are fully agreed: First, it is a dependency relationship, devoid of questioning or critical elements; second, its primary function is one of providing homeostasis among conflicting emotions and impulses, of integrating and stabilizing incongruous fragments of the child's developing self-image; and third, in the course of integrating the child's self-image, it serves as a socializing agent by becoming "as one" with other persons, either parents, older siblings, friends, or teachers. The child assumes not only "the outward manners and expressive movements of these significant figures but attempts also to incorporate their values and attitudes." [95]

Freud takes us one step further by strongly suggesting that, because of the powerful need to establish homeostasis, identification is in fact responsible for transmitting cultural traditions from one generation to the next. This is accomplished by the simple act of the child internalizing the superego of the parent, which includes not only the parent's conscience but his society's norms and institutional beliefs as well. [96]

Although ethologists make no specific reference to identification as being responsible for the transmission of conscience or tradition, there can be no doubt that much of ethological theory is remarkably similar in nature and function. Witness this example from Konrad Lorenz:

> IRMs [Innate Releasing Mechanisms] are inherited mechanisms for the release of a drive in the biologically "correct" situation. They constitute among other things the indispensable prerequisite for the development of a system of higher values. They are likewise impossible to influence through teaching, but some are subject in the course of their development to an imprinting process which accomplishes itself basically on "idols" of the person's own choice. These IRMs the teacher is largely *capable* [Italics added.] of molding, by pointing out suitable examples in history, but above all by his own exemplary conduct. The specific nature of the imprinting process makes it impossible to retrieve an opportunity once neglected and virtually impossible to put right what has once been spoiled.[97]

Because of its implications for teachers, I shall refer to this passage in my discussion of materials and techniques in the final chapter.

If we may trust the exhortations of authorities such as Erikson and Bettelheim, identification also demands the "correct situation" in order for behaviors that we regard as socially and morally acceptable to become properly internalized. Of all the severely disturbed children that come for treatment to Bettelheim's clinic at the University of Chicago, only a few, he tells us, "are suffering from neurosis due to too great attachments to one or both parents, or to an inability to solve conflicts created by those allegiances.... Rather, they are children whose deviate development never gave them a chance to form consistent identifications in the first place. As a result, they have never formed a suitable set of images they could unify in their own minds and use as the model for an integrated personality."[98]

Unfortunately, many new and powerful forces virtually nonexistent a century ago have so radically altered family life-styles that any probability of "correct situations recurring with a certain regularity" is rapidly becoming less favorable than the odds at a Las Vegas gaming table. Ironically, the main culprit is "progress," with special emphasis on our most cherished advances in technology. In former days one means of increasing the probability that the child's internal dynamics will match up with the correct situation was through the extended family, a social arrangement in which all members of a community serve equally as parent figures. This is not to imply that the extended family possesses special skills and knowledge that the nuclear family does not; it merely represents a guarantee of far greater contact between adult and child, thus greatly increasing the chances that meaningful identifications with significant adult figures will occur. Especially in America, technology's role in the disintegration of the extended family has been well documented in the literature of the social scientist. Great mobility, provided by the airplane and the motor car, encourages the breakdown of social interdependence in which children were once unavoidably and intimately involved. Forty years ago, in his *Marriage and Morals*, the principal book that won for him the Nobel Prize in literature, Bertrand Russell pointed out the relationship between the advent of the automobile and the significant increase in the divorce rate. Technology has introduced new forms of recreation, no longer requiring family or community participation. Quietly, steadily, inexorably, each family member, including the child, has transferred his interests and allegiance to the radio, the movie house, and the television set. For parents, in addition, there is the circuit of the plush cocktail lounge, the glittering casino (expanding at an unpredictable rate), and the booming race track—all of which seriously impair the quality and degree of relationship between adult and child. Add to this the fact that a large percentage of mothers of school-age children now work outside the home and you have the ingredients of a social revolution.

In the case of the very young the results have been profoundly disturbing, but for reasons not always thoughtfully analyzed. Of major concern has been the short- and long-term effects of endless hours of exposure to the television set, which has been firmly and irrevocably installed in nearly every American home. While television has been widely touted as a tool for the expansion of learning, much dialogue has been addressed—with considerable ignorance, it seems to me—to the effects of TV violence. Literally thousands of parents, educators, and social critics have made TV a scapegoat. Indeed, it looks as if the whole of America were staging a massive guilt reaction to the problems now besetting youth.

A careful examination of the effects of TV violence, however, poses some major questions that lay critics and researchers alike have not adequately responded to. There seems little doubt, of course, that the original findings of Albert Bandura, D. P. Hartman, Sheila and Dorthea Ross, and others contain a high degree of validity: Exposure to violence does induce antisocial behavior, along with suspected personality malformations.[99] A recent major survey of the literature by Michael Rothenberg at the University of Washington, moreover, strongly corroborates Bandura's conclusions. Going back over the past 25 years of TV viewing, Rothenberg evaluated the hard data found in 50 of the most comprehensive studies involving 10,000 children from every possible background. The relationship between exposure to violence and subsequent aggressive behavior, he found, was a real one—often with lasting results.[100]

The primary weakness of such studies, nonetheless, is their failure to look critically at subsequent behavior in terms of the relationship between what is known about sensitive periods such as identification and the kind of viewing to which the child has been exposed. One might ask, for example, Is TV violence more injurious to children with established patterns of deviate behavior than it is to children who have had opportunities to form suitable sets of images based on positive identifications with significant figures? To what degree do mental processes enter into the act of watching violence? As we have already noted, Piaget, Sears, and even Erikson strongly imply the need of a certain level of intellectual development for identification to function properly. This would suggest, first of all, the making of a choice on the part of the child in order to become "as one" with the object, and second, a consideration of the child's understanding not only of plot and motive—however rudimentary—but his degree of awareness of the object's value system as well.

The condition obviously calls for an analysis of the materials (books, films, TV programs, etc.) to be used with due regard to the child's age and development, and even more specifically a closer look at the word *violence* and the context within which it appears. Perhaps a better choice is the word *conflict*. I strongly propose that, while the internalization of a value system is impossible without identification, conflict as the most universal of all human experiences is a key element in generating the identifying process. I cite as examples two novels that have inspired young readers for many decades: *David Copperfield* and *Treasure Island*. Both are powerful novels of conflict. Although *David Copperfield* lacks violence in a physical sense, the treatment of David by the Murdstones is at times so brutal as to become too unbearable to read. Jim Hawkins (of *Treasure Island*) also is a victim of conflict, some of it violent and bloody, but like David his value system does not include violence as a way of life. As identifying objects I submit that both characters, when properly understood, are far more cleverly calculated to internalize a loathing for violence than an admiration for it.

But technology poses even a far greater threat to the child's development than exposure to violence per se. To fully understand this threat, it is important to mention two factors that seem most predictive of the success or failure of identification as a learning principle. One is the quality of human contact and the other is the length of time in which the principle is allowed to operate. Any extraneous forces altering these two factors are very likely to bring about parallel changes in social behavior.

By far one of the best accounts of how this socializing principle has been profoundly affected by the impact of technology and the consequent altered styles in family life may be found in Urie Bronfenbrenner's comparative studies of American and Russian patterns of child rearing and education (*Two Worlds of Childhood*). In analyzing the two cultures, Bronfenbrenner carefully pinpoints the various influences within each society— mass media, modified family and working habits, enforced peer relations—as they make their impact upon the child. From a background of statistical and empirical evidence relating to essential differences in the children's behavior and to the social forces at work, he was able to diagnose the probable causes with what seems to me remarkable accuracy. All lead up to a startling, carefully documented conclusion directly tied to his major thesis that the health of a nation is not dependent upon the gross national product or the birthrate or the crime statistics, but rather upon "*the concern of one generation for the next.*"[101] Employing cleverly designed measuring instruments, he found that Russian children make significantly more choices favoring adult values than do American children. Such choices, moreover, are far more consistent with acceptable behavior than are those of peer-value-oriented American children, who are more prone to engage in misdemeanors, violence, and other acts of an antisocial nature.[102] Bronfenbrenner readily admits that the pattern among Russian children is rapidly changing because of the same forces that have had such an impact on American life-styles in the past half century.

At first Bronfenbrenner had reason to interpret his findings in terms of a growing tendency in American families toward greater permissiveness in the rearing of children. Later, in the light of new data, he was forced to reassess his position. Although still "consistent with the trend toward permissiveness," the reassessment probed more deeply into the heart of the matter. Of greater significance, Bronfenbrenner reports, was the discovery of a "progressive decrease, especially in recent decades, in the amount of contact between American parents and their children." Among the developed nations of the world, American parents were giving the least amount of their time to the care of their children when children were most in need of it. Technological innovations, with television heading the list, were not only effectively putting an end to any meaningful kind of relationship between parent and child, but also were forcing children into unique peer-group activities, undreamed of or impossible in a former agrarian society. To summarize, "whether in comparison to other contemporary cultures, or to itself over time, American society emerges as one that gives decreasing prominence to the family as a socializing agent.... "[103] From this one may logically infer that, apart from the quality of the child's contact with adults, the degree of the child's allegiance to adult values is directly related to the amount of time in which the identification principle is allowed to operate.

There are moments in the book when Bronfenbrenner apologizes for American parents, suggesting that such behavior is not necessarily a reflection of indifference or neglect or the lack of affection but rather of habit and style evolving from social change. I grant this, to a degree. But with all due respect to the author, whose insight into and knowledge about the American family I greatly admire, I nevertheless find it difficult to overcome a lingering, deeply rooted skepticism. Common sense tells me that a steady erosion of emotional and social contact between parent and child does not make the heart grow fonder or beat faster.

One might reasonably put this down as a calloused point of view were it not for some recent and interesting documentation bearing upon this very issue. Kenneth Keniston, chairman and executive director for the Carnegie Council on Children, explores the question, "Do Americans really like children?" by first enumerating a familiar list of tender sentiments Americans habitually profess about children and then going on to reveal the real story behind the facade. In a society such as ours, which combines social and economic discrimination with the privilege of great wealth, and yet whose affluence is more widespread than anywhere else on earth, it must be presumed that a tangible minority rather than a majority must bear the brunt of deprivation, with its accompanying risks. The presumption is correct. Our children, especially our nonwhite children, make up the bulk of that minority. Keniston cites documentation on the infant mortality rate, nutritional standards (Remember the endless congressional quibbling about free lunches?), equal educational opportunities, and, most important of all, the poverty level and its tragic aftermath, of which nearly a quarter of America's children are victims. In all of these areas we rank below most developed countries enjoying far lower standards of living; in one or two we are truly an undeveloped nation. This, Keniston submits, is not love of children. It is neglect and vast indifference.[104]

Such indifference, together with an economic system that relies heavily on the profit motive, is certainly one of the prime causes of our wider society's inability to achieve any significant kind of acceptance of preadolescent and adolescent youth into the mainstream of American life. The problem this situation creates for youngsters is what Erikson calls *identity and role confusion,* perhaps the second most critical stage of human development in his "Eight Ages of Man." Present to some degree in all societies, identity and role confusion affects particularly the pubescent child, who is suddenly at the mercy of a strange psychological and physiological revolution. He becomes unduly preoccupied with "what he appears to be in the eyes of others as compared with what he feels he is." Puberty is a time when the need to be recognized as a member of the larger society, to be accepted as a part of the future, dominates the youngster's thoughts and most of his activities. His vital link with the future is his "ego identity," which implies, also, a "vocational" identity, for it bears directly on what new role the child sees himself playing, either in fantasy or in fact. In order to acquire a strong and healthy ego identity, the child "must receive consistent, meaningful recognition of his achievements and accomplishments." Without this recognition, role confusion exists and the tendency to identify with peers for the satisfaction of these needs becomes greatly enhanced.[105]

In America, as we know, this is a period in which a youth often struggles in vain to discover who he is, what is his purpose in life, and whether he is important to society. So far as productivity and contributions to the welfare of social units are concerned, no one seems to give a damn whether he is alive or dead. Our public schools, with federal assistance, began responding to this condition some decades ago by establishing departments of home economics, industrial education, agriculture, and other specialized areas at the high school level. These efforts over the long haul have proven abortive, for they speak less to the psychological needs of youth than the economic needs of a capitalistic society. They offer no guarantee of social integration. We may look with amusement or abhorrence at the rite of initiation—some merely superstitious, others painful and barbarous—as practiced in many primitive societies. The fact remains, however, that no social invention has proven more efficacious in guaranteeing youth unqualified passage into adulthood. Strange that ancestral man should have sensed—intuitively, perhaps—the importance of this transitional period not only within its physiological context but its emotional one as well. The emotional component, generated by the enormous collective power of tribal belief and custom, was imperative, for it provided the authentic ring of truth. When all of society announced the advent of adulthood—with its responsibilities and privileges—it was indeed a fact.

Modern societies have neither the will nor the machinery to facilitate this terribly important transformation within our youth. Widespread pluralism and the ambivalence we have noted in American society effectively inhibit an emotional commitment sufficiently broad to convince our young people of its sincerity, while the laws governing our free enterprise system cause business and industry to view the yearly hordes of youth clamoring for vocational identity as a financial threat. Unions endorse prolonged schooling with enthusiasm, fully aware that controlling the numbers within their ranks is consonant with productivity, earning power, and a happy membership. Aware to some degree of what goes on, educators watch from the sidelines, helpless in the grip of social, political, and economic forces over which they exercise little control.

Six

Experiments in Utopia

> *...[I]t is inherent in the human condition that all societies' education will inevitably exact, and thus all societies will pay, a price—a necessary sacrifice—in the coin of developmental crisis and pathology, for their successes in adapting their successive generations to their ways of life.*[106]
>
> —*Melford E. Spiro*

In spite of the limitations enumerated in the previous chapter, I do not wish to imply that the schools' efforts to instill academically and socially desirable attitudes are hopelessly beyond redemption. One of the answers I have repeatedly suggested—an answer that in fact represents the major thesis of this writing—is understanding and employment of the identification principle as a primary socializing agent. For the concluding chapters I should like to examine this principle within the context of two major approaches to education—one involving young children in several differing patterns of organization, the other constituting a fresh look at several important aspects of the teaching act. In developing these ideas, my endeavor is in some degree to "even up the odds," which at present are overwhelmingly stacked against American schools, as they are against society as a whole. For this reason, also, there can be no guaranteed outcomes, since the most fundamental resolutions to problems must ultimately stem from the larger society, of which American schools are currently but a minor though essentially true reflection.

Nor will I deviate from major premises I have already established in this tract. One is my conviction that elements such as *choice, inquiry, discovery, operational truth,* and *consequences,* as they are now implemented in the classroom, are all of one fabric that is basically inimical to social and moral commitment, as well as to the teaching of it, and in the long run far more negative than beneficial in their impact upon children. Moreover, I cannot escape the feeling that they are counterparts of society's growing permissivenesss in child-rearing habits—a permissiveness, incidentally, that appears nowhere in the language of the social scientist describing how desirable attitudes are internalized. In short, I do not believe that the teaching of ethics belongs under the heel of scientific methods, where schools are now trying to put it, and I wonder if this fact, more than any other, will in the future determine the degree of success with which values can be taught in school.

Again I feel the need to point out, as I have earlier, that it is not my intent to denigrate the importance of such strategies as a means of proving, strengthening, implementing, or even modifying *established moral reference points*. But examining a commonly held value is far different from creating one where none previously existed, which has always been my primary interest and concern. I have frequently noted that proponents of "discovery" often exhibit a certain smugness in describing the risk involved with children when, to use a well-worn phrase, the chips are allowed to fall where they may. Progressive-minded teachers, moreover, are forewarned that the condition is one they must be prepared to face, whatever the outcome. This seems to me a dangerous practice, for reasons I shall deal with a bit later.

Another of my major premises is that when a society, either through ignorance or indifference, creates an environment conducive to alienation between generations, the consequences can be devastating. Basically, my concern is the breakdown of identification as an operating principle. The notion deserves a moment's comment. Surely one of the grim aspects in American society, an aspect we have already noted and to which we may no longer close our eyes, is the frightening list of deviant adolescent behaviors reflected by this widening rift between adult and child. While rebellion against adult standards has always characterized youth, it is also true that we must maintain between generations a baseline of mutual respect, communication, and agreement on some very fundamental ways of thinking and acting if social stability is not to be seriously impaired. A growing number of social researchers view any serious deterioration in this relationship as a most alarming state of affairs, irrevocably leading to social disintegration and demise.

Educators have not been entirely oblivious to this growing threat nor to the fact that it is significantly tied to aberrant school attitudes and behaviors. In the late Fifties and Sixties, under the aegis of John Goodlad and like-minded colleagues, they began initiating a number of organizational programs in "open concept," "multigrading," and the like for the purpose of reversing what they felt were several disturbing trends in youth: declining interest in traditional academic content, plummeting achievement scores in the basic skills, and the adoption of strange new life-styles that began openly to flout the staid values and beliefs of the Establishment. The major objective of these programs was ostensibly to improve basic skills, but noncognitive variables also occupied the minds of researchers, especially those dealing with attitudes toward schools and teachers, citizenship, and cultivation of a love of knowledge. Benefits were presumed to emerge from the area of interpersonal relationships. Advocates perceived such arrangements as "natural approximations of family groupings," the ideal of which would include members who range from infants to grandfathers and grandmothers.[107] What allegedly happens is described in the following statement:

> ...[P]upils are motivated academically by those above them and supported emotionally by those below. The psychological processes of socialization and identification are probably facilitated by such an arrangement. Ties of affection and admiration toward younger ones develop. Attitudes, values, and beliefs are extended. Meanwhile, each student is tackling subject matter that fits him, regardless of its grade level.[108]

The sentiment, alas, was rarely destined for fulfillment. My own investigations[109] into these programs and experiments have convinced me that while statistically significant effects of considerable interest to educators often surface from the computerized data,[110] the overall results are by and large anemic, and in many instances they are highly suspect. For one thing, most of the experiments have been peculiarly susceptible to the Hawthorne Effect (merely being the subject of an experiment constitutes a stimulus to achievement) and to a kind of unconscious biasing of procedures and data. Special programs, for example, tend to attract special kinds of teachers, or at the very least to generate teaching behaviors subtly calculated to "prove" the hypotheses, and few accounts I have read have convinced me that this variable was not the most important one in achieving the reported results. There are many studies, moreover, that present opposite claims; enough of them, in fact, to nullify almost every positive statement with a negative one.[111] Perhaps the best illustration of the danger of attaching great importance to such experiments in organization comes from William McLaughlin (*The Nongraded School: A Critical Assessment*), whose analysis of 32 major research findings forcibly convinced him that the evidence was "ambiguous" at best, "inconclusive" at worst.[112]

There is, in addition, damaging evidence regarding children's ability to establish any stable relationship between responsible independence and humane social cohesion without *early and continuous adult intervention.*[113] Obviously, how any one child will be affected by the group must depend on the social and moral climate prevailing within that group. If the group's norms encourage mutual trust and cooperation, one may expect children to behave accordingly; where they call for repeated violation of adult rules and standards, these too will be swiftly translated into action. As it has in the past, recent literature provides us with a chilling example of this truth. I refer to William Golding's *Lord of the Flies*, written in 1955.[114] When a group of pre-adolescent boys are marooned on an island and left to their own devices, their partially internalized norms break down under the shift to peer power and tyranny, leaving in its wake the brutal slaying of Piggy, one of the group members. The act occurs just prior to the arrival of adult rescuers, whose very first question upon discovery of the body is: "Are there any adults—any grownups with you?"

The implication is clear, but perhaps it is most succinctly expressed in the words of Bronfenbrenner:

> If adults do not once again become involved in the lives of children, there is trouble ahead for American society. New patterns of life have developed in our culture. One result of these changes has been the reduced participation of adults in the socialization of children. Although, to date, this pattern has continued to gain acceptance, there is reason to believe that it can do harm to our children and to our society. We are therefore faced with the necessity of developing a new style of socialization, one that will correct inadequacies of our contemporary pattern of living as it is affecting our children and provide them with opportunities for humanizing experiences of which they are now bereft.[115]

When Bronfenbrenner speaks of a "new style of socialization," he is in fact urging American educators and parents to look critically at some unique aspects of the Russian day-care programs, which we have already mentioned in passing, and of which he has made an exhaustive scientific study. I would add to these a number of important approaches found in the Israeli kibbutz experiments as reported by Bruno Bettelheim[116] and Melford E. Spiro.[117] In contrast to our own experiments with the open concept and multigrading, both Russian and Israeli forms offer some provocative insights into our own educational planning for the future—at least in terms of alternatives deserving careful examination.

Although there are important differences between the two educational patterns that space does not allow me to explore fully, the similarities are of primary interest. Both, for example, employ the "collective" setting for the upbringing and teaching of children—a unique system in which peer-group contact becomes the major influence in character formation. This means, in effect, that children are separated from parents very early in life—generally a few months after birth—and placed, according to age, in various houses or dormitories from whence they move from infancy through high school in small groups under the supervision of carefully chosen caretakers, nurses, teachers, and other professional personnel. In the kibbutz setting parents visit their children but do not live with them, while Russian children are brought home in the late afternoon or evening and are returned to the designated house early the next morning. It would be wrong to assume that in both instances contact between parents and children is minimal. Actually, in terms of contact hours, it is considerably longer than in most Western countries and particularly longer than in the United States. Of equal significance, it is also more intimate and emotion laden, involving words of endearment, much cuddling, and other physical handling, especially in Russia.

Differences in approach stem primarily from the national character. In seeking greater independence for its children, kibbutz upbringing is more permissive in a wide range of behaviors, including such things as toilet training, table manners, freedom to criticize, and a respect for physical labor in preference to intellectual achievement. Competition in school is studiously avoided.

Russian training is more structured and disciplined, with stronger political and intellectual orientation. Competition is not only encouraged but employed in such a way as to cause Russian children to vie with each other in the perpetuation of political goals and values. Propaganda at the national level is unique in giving to teachers and other professional caretakers broad support that works powerfully in their influence over children. This is accomplished through huge parades announcing the advent of the new school year, lauding teachers as national heros, and directing all avenues of the media to the task of inculcating children with the notion that the teacher and education are the most important things in their lives. Children are virtually trapped within a carefully planned environment in which specific responses are all but unavoidable.

In both environments, children are always physically close to adults, often visiting their places of work and actively participating in many of their personal and social functions, thus insuring that values are passed on by the entire community: parents, relatives, teachers, nurses, and other adult figures. In both cultures, finally, there is a conspicuous absence of the burgeoning antisocial behavior that marks so many of our own youth, while intellectual interests and activity appear to be considerably higher.[118]

Whatever view we may hold regarding these approaches to child rearing, when it comes to the schools' responsibility for furthering our democratic way of life, we face the same scientific problem that American researchers on kibbutz education addressed themselves to: "...[I]t is not whether collective education is good or bad.... The problem is: What...forces find their un-noted expression in the forms of collective education, and how do these forms of upbringing induce behavior forms (social modalities) and behavior problems which in their genetic sequence result in individuals who perpetuate the way of the life of the kibbutz?"[119] We may not approve of the philosophy underlying their stated goals or the means by which these goals are implemented, but we cannot argue with the predictability of the results. For, contrary to our own increasingly uncertain outcomes in education, the Russian and kibbutz child-rearing patterns do "result in individuals" who perpetuate their own carefully planned societies.

In America, also, schools are regarded, among other things, as instruments for transferring social and political ideals across the generations. In the United States, one might say, the objective is to discover means of continuously achieving these ideals in a milieu of social cohesion that not only prohibits undue repression but also allows children some life of impulse. Obviously, the success of this important function calls for the creation of a certain amount of allegiance between young and old. The leading question then is, Why do peer-group influences—strongly and increasingly present in all three cultures—act as a stimulus to the acceptance of adult values in Russia and Israel while producing the opposite effect in the U. S.?

The answer, it seems to me, is both simple and complex. The simple answer is that both Russia and Israel provide structured training to peer groups, or, to put it into Skinnerian terms, they arrange a closely controlled and limited environment to which children may respond, whereas the United States does not. As Bronfenbrenner has suggested, "the peer group is heavily—perhaps too heavily—influenced by adult society. In contrast, the American peer group is relatively autonomous, cut off from the adult world—a particularly salient example of segregation by age."[120] The complexity of the answer is inherent in our way of life. Let us grant that the solution lies in providing specific kinds of stimuli, the nature of which we already understand fairly well. Then the question becomes, How, in the face of a bewildering array of counteracting forces, do we carry out the task of implementation?

However monumental these difficulties, our only recourse appears to be one that Skinner has repeatedly attempted to convey to the American public in general and the educational segment in particular. He tells us that only through environmental engineering can we hope to produce individuals who will guarantee the continuation of those democratic freedoms that detractors claim his methods are designed to destroy. Whatever the case, I view as examples of invincible ignorance those critics whose response to this kind of control invariably becomes a catechism on the evils of conformity and the consequent destruction of individuality. By promoting this concept of some god-like "autonomous man," they take pride in turning a dangerous vice into a virtue, oblivious to society's frequent need for concerted group action. A philosophy stating that a person can maintain both his personal identity and his commitment to society without ever having to sacrifice one for the other is bound to generate serious problems in the decision-making process—a condition that has effectively prohibited any hope of a national commitment to our children. I think it was Bertrand Russell who observed that, invariably, men with an overinflated sense of individualism were peculiarly unfit to agree upon anything but matters of the most trifling significance.

In the final analysis we must take note of Spiro's warning that there is risk in whatever course we pursue. Without exception, every society, he points out, will exact a toll of its children in terms of developmental crisis and pathology in its efforts to regenerate its own way of life. The cost of the kibbutz style of collectivism, he adds, is "no larger than the price which the products of most systems must pay for the privilege of becoming human—and it is smaller than many."[121] Before judging too harshly, we should keep in mind that we, too, are paying a price, but with steadily diminishing assurance that this staggering cost will guarantee our future as a democratic nation.

One comes away from such accounts with a strong belief that organizational patterns are truly effective when they are imposed on extremely young children—age 2 or younger—when the behavior of parents, teachers, and other caretakers represents many hours of direct and emotionally supportive contact, and when the environment is carefully controlled. Such criteria are in a sense an oversimplification, to be sure, for they say nothing of the vast range and variety of techniques involved. Nevertheless, I am convinced that they constitute the essential elements which will determine any society's success or failure in adapting its future generations to a particular way of life.

They are surely the elements that will determine the fate of our own programs such as Head Start, early childhood education, and others of a similar nature. Head Start, if we may believe Kenneth Keniston, is in serious trouble because of its shift to a strong intellectual base (a trend in education I have mentioned several times in passing) aimed at raising the IQs of culturally deprived children. Although improving intellectual achievement was one of the objectives of Head Start, its main purpose was to give new "power to parents, to broaden the experience of children in noncognitive ways, and provide them with many services such as health and dental care."[122] As it turns out, the real "value and progress" of these children has been "judged primarily by their capacity to do well on tests of intelligence, reading readiness, or school achievement."[123]

True or not, full credit must be given to Keniston for his insight into what is likely the most fundamental of causes that effectively destroy any effort, however worthy or sophisticated, to raise these children to higher levels of socialization. I quote at length from his highly perceptive article, "Do Americans *Really* Like Children?"

> The fashionable theory underlying much of the valuation of Head Start attributes the plight of those children to something called "cultural deprivation." I'll concede that this is one way of looking at the situation, but it seems to me that we need to get at what is *causing* the cultural deprivation. It is certainly easy to see that the term *culturally deprived* has come to be just another euphemism for poor and/or black. And it seems clear to me, at least, that the reason some families cannot provide their children with intellectual stimulation at breakfast and cultural riches at dinner is that they are blighted by and bogged down in poverty.
>
> Now I, for one, see poverty as a manifestation, not of our cultural system, but of our economic system. So I suggest that it is extremely odd to speak of cultural deprivation as the primary problem facing destitute families, whether in inner-city ghettos or in impoverished Appalachian hollows.[124]

Apart from the effects of an economy that must ultimately be reckoned with, our fondest hopes for raising our children's IQ levels or insuring the most rudimentary kinds of character development will in the main prove to be a fantasy unless we are able to control those sensitive variables that social scientists have identified as being most crucial to *any* pattern of child rearing and education; to wit, a guarantee of *appropriate* physical and emotional experiences between birth and puberty, continuous supervision of and participation in children's lives, and a *selectively* limited environment. That these are elements that researchers have found to be most prominent in the two collective settings we have briefly examined makes them no less critical in their application.

The success or failure of our ongoing programs in early childhood education are bound by precisely the same criteria. If we are correctly interpreting the data available from the Russian and kibbutz experiments, early childhood education, as developed within the state of California, for example, may well represent an effort that is too little and too late, unless psychologically tied to pre-existing day-care programs: too little

63

in its ability to control the variables we have discussed, too late in terms of the child's age at the point of entry. I do not question that many positive aspects emerging from the program— especially those cited by State Superintendent Wilson Riles—are both valid and hold promise for the future. But I would venture that the documented successes rest far less upon the introduction of "new teacher roles," "staff retraining," "operating, monitoring, evaluating," etc., than upon Riles's unique talents for infusing high community interest and especially generating *enormously increased adult participation,* thus allowing identification and conditioning principles to do their work.[125]

By the same token, the "back to basics" movement, along with its huge bandwagon syndrome, simply cannot survive without the effective intervention of these principles. I am amused at the naiveté of communities, school boards, and even educators who delude themselves into believing that a revival of the so-called basics is predicated upon 1) the elimination of frill courses, 2) the resurrection of old-fashioned discipline, 3) a return to the three Rs, 4) a resumption of homework, and 5) the introduction of competency-based testing to determine a student's qualification for going on to higher levels of learning. One is led to believe that good teaching is a brand-new discovery emerging out of the late Seventies!

Such methods are helpful, to be sure, but what improved achievement scores truly represent is the community's ability to create a special "climate" for children, a climate that effectively screens out distracting or competing stimuli from the child's world, surrounding him with an aura of intense belief that can only be generated by the power of total adult commitment. The resulting condition is one in which children's behaviors are funneled into academically and skill-oriented avenues of endeavor from which, quite literally speaking, there is no escape.

To put it another way, insuring the internalization of specific modes of behavior is a matter of limiting, within a framework of continuous supervision and emotional support, children's options by selection rather than offering them free choices. The evil or good that ensues from the process is a question for Americans as philosophers to decide. Should they conclude that certain approaches to child rearing and education contain elements detrimental to our democratic institutions (if these are in fact what Americans wish to perpetuate), then, by means of arranging different "environmental contingencies," as Skinner would put it, they must set a new kind of stage for the coming of the next generation. What appears certain is that there must be consensus on the needs of society and youth and sufficient adult involvement to fulfill these needs if anything is to alter the uncertain course upon which we are now embarked.

Seven

In Search of Pygmalion

If further research showed that it is possible to find teachers whose untrained educational style does for their pupils what our teachers did for the special children, the prospect would arise that a combination of sophisticated selection of teachers and suitable training of teachers would give all children a boost toward getting as much as they possibly can out of their schooling.[126]

—*Robert Rosenthal*

Because there is little evidence that education in America will soon move in directions consistent with national policy and commitment, I shall focus my attention on the implications my own reading and experience may have for the nature of the teaching act itself—that is, the teacher, his instructional materials, and his methods.

First, the teacher. The teacher as an instrument of change in student behavior has been the object of a great deal of frustration in past years for researchers and educators alike. During the Fifties and early Sixties there was a great rash of experiments initiated to find significant relationships between teacher characteristics and various aspects of academic achievement and social behavior. With a few exceptions, the programs gradually dwindled for lack of hard evidence. Such experiments, moreover, were often very expensive, and growing disenchantment with the results caused most funding sources to dry up.[127]

At about the same time, sweeping social changes had started a major shift in emphasis. Civil rights movements and subsequent legislation were redirecting the center of attention from teachers to programs: urban center programs, migrant programs, culturally oriented programs, programs to break down language barriers, programs for the economically deprived—all with considerable infusions of money. The target was no longer selection or the search for those elements that separate talent from mediocrity but new techniques, retraining, cultural sensitivity, and a giant expansion of instructional materials and facilities.

As a result, the methods of screening candidates for the teaching profession remain essentially unchanged—which means that policies for admission into schools of education throughout America rest primarily on three factors: 1) a professed desire to teach, 2) a minimum grade-point average, and 3) the ability to move one's body.* For several decades now, schools of education have continued to bumble along, firmly entrenched in the belief that course work of a startling variety and nature will provide answers to any problem. They remain oblivious to the message of social scientists whose investigations make it increasingly clear that the acquired expertise in dealing with the young child may not be nearly as critical to the child's development as a teaching style that is unlearned. They fail to create possibilities for teachers who are potentially the most powerful influences in the child's life to realize their full potential.

Although these facts point irrevocably toward a more sophisticated method of selecting candidates and, further, providing them with a status that functions powerfully not only within the school but also within the child's home, education departments are either stymied by lack of manageable data on how to proceed, or—even more seriously—they are motivated by factors in the present economy that spell out survival or extinction. Consider for a moment: Publicly supported higher institutions of learning throughout America are becoming increasingly subject to the funding policies of state legislators whose only hope for reelection is based on a hard-nosed platform of accountability resulting from the shrinking tax dollar. Meanwhile, few departments have been harder hit by declining enrollment than professional education; when justification for their existence becomes totally dependent on the generation of credit hours, the consequences are painfully obvious. Assuming that schools of education were inclined to apply more stringent criteria to their currently minimal screening practices, the increased drop in enrollment, together with staff RIF and highly probable department closures, would surely act as a powerful deterrent.

Even the thought of such desperate measures is enough to precipitate severe intellectual disorientation. As state superintendents of public instruction—carrying out the will of legislators—set down more and more difficult mandates, education departments begin reacting like whirling dervishes in a ritual dance of frenzied activity with little substance. Suddenly, the preoccupation with credit hours turns into an all-consuming passion. Professors become expert purveyors of all the traditional content areas, including dozens that until recently never existed. Endless hours of brainstorming result in a profusion of lofty and impractical ideals destined for the trashheap, or in bizarre organizational configurations, with definition layered upon definition, qualification upon qualification—all of which in-

---

*There are some minor exceptions to this practice, i.e., minimum competency tests in reading, spelling, mathematics, and so on.

66

variably ends in a conceptual quagmire.

Curiously, there is little if any disenchantment with the outcome. Year after year, otherwise intelligent men and women take obvious pleasure in stirring up the same dunghill. Indeed, it is as if the effects were strongly hypnotic, lulling members into a grateful dreamlike state in which all is made well with the world by the mere act of repetition. When, upon occasion, deeply concerned teachers are invited to join these sessions, they stare in disbelief. "What in God's name," they ask themselves, "has all this to do with selecting and training good teachers?"*

The judgment is a harsh one, to be sure, and perhaps ought to be softened by the fact that departments of education, like public schools, are also victims of a Catch-22 situation in which delegated power to resolve social and academic problems is effectively nullified by the same forces that create the problems. Nevertheless, in their present love affair with "competency," "accountability," and other performance criteria (yesterday it was "behavioral objectives" and "sensitivity training"),** it would be virtually impossible to initiate a search for the kind of candidate whose *natural* teaching style is most consistent with our documented hypothesis that *because identification is a factor of major dimension in any educational pursuit, a teacher's ability to establish an atmosphere most conducive to its operation is crucial.* Such an atmosphere, moreover, is achieved only through a number of uniquely *human* characteristics within the teacher. This sounds harmless enough but in fact contains ramifications that, when considered in their entirety, may be sources of embarrassment and trepidation to administrators and school board members alike.

Within our framework of options, if this teacher were to possess but two dominant traits, they would be his spirit of reverence for children and his unbounded conviction that every child is capable of reaching his (the child's) full potential. While these are qualities that hiring personnel widely subscribe to in theory, they make little effort in practice to insure their presence in the candidate and often give higher priority to glibness,*** scholarship, and organizational ability. Yet, if we accept the views of the eminent analyst, Erich Fromm, the first of these qualities not only stands as the single most important ingredient within the teacher's repertoire of personal characteristics but is one which our own materialistic culture has largely ignored. In his own words, "While we teach knowledge,

---

*The statement is not mere speculation; it is based on numerous conversations with teachers who have attended such planning sessions, both at my institution and at others.

**As lovers, departments of education are outrageously fickle, constitutionally incapable of separating true beauty from what is merely skin-deep.

***Especially during interviews.

we are losing that teaching which is the most important one for human development: the teaching which can only be given by the simple presence of a mature, loving person. In previous epochs of our own culture, or in China and India, the man most highly valued was the person with outstanding spiritual qualities. Even the teacher was not only, or even primarily, a source of information, but his function was to convey certain human attitudes....''[128]

The second quality is based on a long-established but only superficially regarded truth, that when high expectations of children's ability to learn are consistently and sincerely demonstrated through teaching behavior, such expectations are in fact largely fulfilled. It was demonstrated in an experiment by Robert Rosenthal[129] during which a group of teachers were led to believe that certain of their children (randomly chosen) were potentially high achievers. As a consequence, these children—especially at first- and second-grade levels—rose significantly in IQ and basic skills above their counterparts, a matched control group about whom the teachers had received no such information.*

The significance of this study lies in what Rosenthal called the "untrained educational style," a concept whose implications for selecting teacher candidates are virtually without precedent. That a group of teachers, totally without prompting or special training, were able to do what they did simply because a conviction had been firmly implanted in their minds is nothing less than startling. It is, by all counts, an outstanding example of how the power of belief may reflect itself in a whole series of unusually sensitive and perceptive behaviors toward children—behaviors that remain largely outside the province of explicit training.

of themselves always do the job; they are frequently too passive in character. As Rosenthal has suggested, the element of *suitable training* would be a highly desirable ingredient. To be specific, what is needed is the addition of certain talents that may serve somewhat the same function as catalytic agents in a chemical reaction. High among these is the teacher as dramatist, not in the sense of the accomplished actor but as one skillfully trained to recognize those parts of the curriculum that lend themselves to dramatic treatment. I am not suggesting that we abandon the teaching of rational processes but simply that we place them whenever possible within an emotional context, employing such elements as narrative, conflict, and denouement. If we are still talking about attitudes, we must face a fact of life that all the *hard* evidence (social and psychological) seems to point to: In order for

---

*While the Rosenthal experiment has been questioned by other researchers, the findings have been successfully defended by Rosenthal and his associates.

attitude formation to occur, *teachers must espouse the arguments that favor the attitudes or beliefs we wish to instill.* Again, if this appears to be an arbitrary view suggestive of indoctrination, we should perhaps reexamine the attitude or belief in question, or even abandon our efforts in this area entirely. What exerts the greatest impact on children's attitudes is not that their intelligence is exposed to reason, but that children are exposed to dynamic teachers.

In an age of vast social change and upheaval, the teacher as social critic is indispensable to the program. The notion that small children cannot identify with social issues involving the most fundamental human rights is sheer nonsense. Awakening children to feelings and attitudes that are often couched in sophisticated language is not easy; but it is not impossible. What child has not felt the sting of rejection by his classmates or teacher through no fault of his own, or the panic fear that comes from having voiced an unpopular opinion, or the bitterness of isolation in a contest of unequal opportunity? These, it seems to me, are the very stuff on which human rights are built.

The teacher must also possess the temper of the liberal mind if his presence before children is not to exemplify a highly dogmatic and opinionated view of life. By the liberal attitude I mean one that is trusting and accepting of others, however bizarre their ideas or appearance, and unfearful of losing face when found wrong. It is the attitude that in turn enables children to express themselves, not anarchistically but fearlessly, so that they need not build insular detachments and hostilities in defense of their own errors, which so often leads to the narrow, prejudiced outlook. The learner whose responses are purposely disruptive, or who maintains frigid silence, is the product of teachers (and parents) who have themselves too often cringed helplessly under the lash of adult scorn—almost invariably the scorn of the typical authoritarian.

Except for the temper of liberalism, which is sometimes sadly lacking in the very youth whose courage and dedication we so much admire, the teacher we speak of might well be drawn from the ranks of articulate young radicals. He might be something of a firebrand, uncomfortable to live with, a bane to his principal but a joy to his children, who see him as the champion of their own unredressed grievances against the adult world.

Somewhat earlier we spoke of the need for establishing and maintaining a baseline of fundamental relationships between generations, without which a society cannot for long survive. Although the preschool environment is unquestionably the single most influential factor in developing it, I am convinced that the teacher I have just described is the most likely candidate for constructively affecting these relationships, at least in part. Is he anywhere to be found? Again, my convictions tell me "yes," and that the means of identifying him are logically implied in the experimental procedures described by researchers such as Rosenthal, Spiro, and Bronfenbrenner, and in Albert Bandura's extensive explorations into modeling.

The technique of single and multiple modeling, for example, demands attention, for it utilizes identification as its key operating principle. Having carefully evaluated Bandura's data, Bronfenbrenner, in particular, is convinced that modeling carries provocative implications for educational and social programs. Contrary to the criteria established by most professional educators, however, he rates *teacher status* as the most essential quality in the relationship between teacher and child. Indeed, in order for the "teacher...to function as an effective model and reinforcer, she must possess the characteristics which we have identified as enhancing inductive power; that is, she must be perceived by pupils as a person of status who has control over resources...."[130] What this seems to indicate is that children are sensitive to teachers not only in terms of their own personal contacts but also in their perceptions of the teacher's relationship to his nonteaching environment, i.e., his image as a figure of authority, the respect paid him by others, and the like.*

However we may choose to assess this factor, it is an interesting, perhaps extremely significant, alternative to the criteria that have traditionally occupied the minds of educators, and it may well make up an important part of Rosenthal's concept of the teacher's "untrained educational style." Unlike the investigations of the Fifties and Sixties that tried, futilely, to find a link between teacher characteristics and student achievement, the researchers I have mentioned appear to be interested in discovering those environmental factors—teaching behaviors included—that cause children to identify more strongly with their peers than with the adult world. Within this concept, they believe, lies the major solution to some of education's thorniest problems, either cognitive or noncognitive. Its investigation, moreover, calls for new experimental approaches that should rank among the highest priorities to which educators may address themselves.

---

*It should not escape us that these are the very same elements that frequently influence our own perceptions of our fellow man.

Eight

Can Teaching Make a Difference?

*It [Highet's book] is called **The Art of Teaching** because I believe that teaching is an art, not a science. It seems to me very dangerous to apply the aims and methods of science to human beings as individuals.... Of course it is necessary for any teacher to be orderly in planning his work and precise in his dealing with facts. But that does not make teaching "scientific." Teaching involves emotions, which cannot be systematically appraised and employed, and human values, which are quite outside the grasp of science....*[131]

—Gilbert Highet

For the teacher deeply concerned with children's attitudes toward the world they live in, the style and content of much of today's elementary curriculum, as well as the methods of teaching it, must be disappointing. Except for a small but growing volume of library fiction, the reading that takes up so large a part of the child's school time is quite devoid of all but the most innocuous kinds of social learning. The readers, especially at the lower elementary levels, are still largely occupied with community helpers, lost pets, animal characters, and trite mysteries. Apart from the occasional classic or story written by the established writer, their only claim to drama is that they employ the technique of dialogue, whose banalities are frequently matched only by those of the plot. Much of a child's life is involved with misplaced puppies and make-believe journeys to the moon, but these cannot be the whole of it. Deep attachments, deep loss, hate, fear, rivalry, and revenge are as much a part of his life as they are of the adult's.

In response to the discovery that children of minority groups were conspicuously absent from the literary world of the white middle-class child, publishers are now hastening to fill in the gap. As we flip through the pages of their latest edition, we find increasing numbers of illustrations that begin to look suspiciously like characters from Negro, Chinese, and Mexican families.[132] But although their eyes are slanted or their skins dark, one would never dream that the minority child had a single problem that was significantly, or even mildly, different from his white classmate's. Together they walk the shaded streets of suburbia, wearing the same clothes and playing the same games. Inside bright new homes they enjoy sumptuous holiday dinners and lavish yuletide gifts—all remarkably similar. There is no anguish or pain. Segregation, isolation, racism—indeed, anything that smacks of the privation or privilege found in the lives of real children—have been carefully deleted from their world, leaving it sparkling, aseptic, and trouble-free.

Elementary social studies suffer from a different kind of illness, but lead essentially to the same result. Expository writing, concept building, and the integration of new disciplines dominate their pages to the exclusion of social themes that, if mentioned at all, receive but scant attention. This does not mean that they lack scholarship. Indeed, the author with the Ph.D. in history appears with increasing frequency on the title pages. The one criticism we cannot make is their want of dedication to their own brand of truth.

Perhaps the most prestigious example of such truth was the publication, not too long ago, of a series of instructional materials entitled *Man: A Course of Study,* that was adopted in many elementary schools in America. The presumption here, as formulated by the eminent psychologist Jerome Bruner, is that in order to help children discover what makes man human, they must be exposed to instruction in the science of behavior rather than to history. While there is much that is fascinating to children in *Man: A Course of Study,* I am not convinced that a study of the life cycle of salmon, herring gulls, and baboons is especially helpful in showing children that what truly distinguishes man from other animals is his potential for moral behavior, or that we need go outside the record of our own behavior to learn it, if it can be learned at all.

While truth in the pursuit of teaching is a matter of grave importance, equally important for young children is the style or manner in which truth is presented. The significance of style reverts directly to Konrad Lorenz's counsel on the importance of historical models as imprinting objects and to the fact that identification also occurs through fantasy or, to use the literary term, through vicarious experience. To illustrate this point I should like to cite from my own experience. A number of years ago, while engaged in writing a textbook for children in the elementary grades, I conceived the notion of telling the Northwest Indian story in terms of ruthless exploitation by the whites and the Indian's reaction to the swift destruction of his culture. To do this I described him briefly as he appeared at the coming of the white man: generous, cunning, childishly naive yet cleverly resourceful—a being filled with purpose and with deep pride in his ways. As his time began to run out, however, he was presented through the eyes of several pioneer historians who had observed him at firsthand as a human derelict cast away in small groups on some desolate stretch of beach, embittered by broken promises, sick and debauched by the white man's disease and bad whiskey. Landless and spiritually corrupted, he had lost all purpose and dignity.

Needless to say, my efforts were gently though firmly rebuffed. Such an approach, I was told, was not in good taste. For one thing it was too brutal for children of this tender age. For another, it was overly pessimistic.

Well, I had never supposed that it wasn't. But history, I knew, was on my side; the facts were there for anyone who wanted to examine them. Besides, I have always felt that a certain amount of guilt is salutary.* I wondered if the unvarnished truth might not help instill in our children some sense of outrage at the enormous moral wrongs for which every white being on earth must assume a measure of responsibility. I was not unaware of our moments of greatness—of those noble acts of sacrifice and generosity that are also a part of the record. But it seemed to me the fine things have always found ways of getting themselves publicized, while the ugly ones are more often swept under the rug. I wondered if it were not more fitting that our children walk in the shadow of humility than in the glare of overweening pride. I felt that the record was in need of better balancing.

But if this avenue was barred, I was encouraged to find others. Indeed, a sympathetic treatment of the Indian was not only desirable but imperative, and I had only to find a more acceptable way of showing what a fine fellow he was. The solution finally pointed out to me was through the development of "concepts," a theme familiar to every writer of elementary text materials. In this instance the Indian is observed in close harmony with nature as he plays out his role as hunter, artisan, family man, and, occasionally, warrior. Out of the materials emerge the conceptual relationships between Indian art and religion, climate and culture, man and nature's resources, and so on. Except for patches of artificial dialogue intended to stimulate interest, the style is expository, with great stress on organization and vocabulary control. It is, as one might suspect, a style that lends itself exceedingly well to dullness, rising occasionally to power, but limited for the most part by the treatment of the materials.

I sighed in resignation and went to work. My own examination of sample elementary texts preparatory to writing, together with my own teaching experience, should have taught me that social

---

*It is reassuring to know that when all of America seems bent on purging itself of guilt through conflict resolution techniques, sensitivity groups, est, etc., Harvard psychiatrist Robert Coles wonders why there isn't more of it around. "Is our job really to attenuate people's guilts," he asks, "or would it be a better world if some of us were a little more guilty and conflicted?" "What About Moral Sensibility?" *Today's Education*, September/October, 1971, p. 41.

studies at this level are strongly materialistic in bias and that social ideas, except as they are treated innocuously on the community-helper level, are practically nonexistent. The feeling, apparently, is that ideas of this caliber must await greater development of reflective powers before much can be done with them.

Another example of the standard treatment of the Indian may be found in my second textbook for children, written several years later. By this time I had learned my lesson well and proceeded immediately to pay proper deference to Chief Joseph and his tribe for having been badly used by our government. In the space of a few pages children learn all the "objective" facts about our comparative cultures, Joseph's brilliance as an Indian general, and his retirement onto a reservation, "a wise and gentle leader of his people."[133] Interesting as these facts might be, they might well have been left unsaid. Of infinitely more importance for the young child's mind is that Chief Joseph should serve as a symbol of our treatment of minority groups. In this use of history, children glimpse the haunting loveliness of the Wallowa Valley, the ancestral home of the Nez Perce tribe. They observe the incredible greed of miners and pioneers, followed by swift encroachment, dishonored treaties, and a long list of indignities which at last force upon Joseph his momentous decision to fight.

While his remarkable generalship in a long series of running battles is high drama, its chief importance lies in the specific details. Children should know something of Chief Joseph's anguish as he watches the slow and systematic extermination of his people. Through his eyes and ears they should be made to look upon defenseless women and children put to the sword by U.S. troops and hear the children's whimpering cries of hunger, pain, and cold as the embattled tribe, ever on the move, fights its way over 1,500 tortuous miles of wilderness in advance of the pursuing U.S. Army. Perhaps then they might gain some understanding of the tragic depth of Chief Joseph's resignation and bitterness as he makes his surrendering speech—one of the most simple and moving in Indian oratory: "I am tired of fighting. Our chiefs are killed. Looking Glass is dead. Tu-hul-hut-sut is dead. The old men are all dead.... It is cold and we have no blankets. The little children are freezing to death. I want to have time to look for my children and see how many of them I can find. Maybe I shall find them among the dead. Hear me, my chiefs.... From where the sun now stands I will fight no more forever."[134]

Nor should children be spared the last act of perfidy in this drama, when our government, in violation of the solemn pledge upon which Chief Joseph laid down his arms, condemns him and the tattered remnant of his tribe to a strange and hostile environment nearly 2,000 miles away, where eight years of neglect and disease reduce his small group to a tiny handful.

For small children this is one of a number of precious themes in a great heritage involving man's continuing battle for human rights. What a pity to squander it as we do. The fact that it shames our honor makes it no less significant, but rather more so. How else can we develop in our children a sense of national conscience? What better way to insure that such barbarism, of which our government is from time to time capable, should never happen again?

It is curious that those branches of the federal government that so generously dispense their largess on a confusing array of research projects have never enlisted the aid of the gifted dramatist to help write the curriculum for the needs of the child's emotional world. Because, frankly, the fulfillment of such needs lies more within the province of the literary arts than in that of the social studies, and it is perhaps time the social studies began to borrow seriously from them. I am not talking about the trappings and papier-mache models of literature with which so much elementary social studies writing was once—and to some degree still is—invested. This is the world of synthetic plots, of taking tours to zoos, museums, and department stores, of returning to the classroom where children chatter blithely about what they have seen. I speak of genuine literary talent, which includes the all-important sense of drama, a sharp eye for detail, and the ability to turn little words—*dramatically*—into big ideas with emotional impact. These are the qualities needed to breathe life into human events in which powerful moral values are at stake.

But such an assessment, I am aware, points irrevocably to a major reconstruction in the social studies program for children. I see no other way. This subject at all levels has been for too long conceived and taught in a moral vacuum. Yet if science has told us anything at all about small children, it is that the "sensitive period" in a child's life is a very precious thing. Unlike the period for other kinds of learning, which ends only with death, its time grows fleeting and must be nurtured in its own way if it is not to become irretrievably lost. For never again will this child identify so keenly with the vicissitudes of his significant figures and groups. Never will he feel so intensely their despair at injustice, brutality, and intolerance, nor accept so uncritically their own shining virtues. Horatio Alger may have given his countless readers a version of the American success story as phony as a three-dollar bill, but I, for one, am still unable to disembarrass myself completely of the idea that industry, like cleanliness, is next to Godliness. The curious thing is that the characters and events have long since faded from memory.

In practical terms I envision a social and moral drama of conflict, a goodly portion of which would deal with the unsung protagonists of history. Having experimented briefly with this form in my own writings for children, I am aware that the results would not always be acceptable to book publishers whose offerings are now so heavily overshadowed by the mystique of concept building, inquiry learning, and the addition of new content areas. And of course it would surely mean that the white world, from the sixteenth century onward, would emerge something less than perfect.

But no matter. It is the unique idea involved here that counts—a phenomenon commonly described as the story of the underdog, whose powers are as strange as those that lurk in Freud's world of the unconscious. Well known to literature, it is oblivious to color, race, creed, or religion, paying its allegiance only to someone or some group in pursuit of a cause. The cause may be lost or won, but the re-enactment of it always involves a struggle against great odds.

B. F. Skinner remarks on this unusual phenomenon with keen perception. Behavior that is either directed, instructed, or imitated, he tells us, elicits little interest in the observer or reader, even though it may lead to beneficial results. After all, who cares about the success story of a person who has been carefully prompted each step of the way by some external agency? But try placing in front of the same protagonist great obstacles that he attempts to overcome *through his own resources,* especially when the odds are heavily stacked against him. How different the reaction! Now we are suddenly caught up in a wish-fulfilling process that stems directly from our own inadequacies and unrequited strivings toward personal goals.[135] Harking back to the time of tribal fires and the teller of tales, it is a condition as ancient as man himself.

Because of the great power they can wield over the hearts and minds of children, the methods of the teacher himself must in a large sense resemble those of the teller of tales. For example, I cannot conceive of any teacher helping children to internalize the democratic virtues with real effectiveness unless he is a shrewd and vocal critic of the current scene, constantly invoking from the past and the world of today those examples of behavior that bear upon our historically developed ideals of justice and fair play. But invoking examples is not enough. He must learn to do this within the context of drama and drama's most formidable weapon: conflict and subsequent anger.

Dramatizing instructional materials is not a question of learning how to declaim or deliver panegyrics. Drama, when defined, is more properly the art of presenting subject matter in terms of opposing forces. Surprisingly, the technique accommodates itself to a broad range of content areas, an example of which first came to my notice a number of years ago while I awaited an appointment in an attorney's office. I had picked up a magazine and opened it at random to a short piece on wild flowers, the most unlikely of subjects. Fifteen or 20 minutes later I realized, to my surprise, that I had read the whole article intently without pause. Because wild flowers had never rated high on my inventory of interests, I quickly reread the article, curious to know how the author had tricked me into reading to the very end.

The answer was immediately apparent. The writer had used the technique of the dramatist by portraying the wild flower in opposition to its pampered cousin, the domesticated flower. How was it, he asked his readers, that the domestic variety, in spite of its lush beauty and sturdy appearance, would never last out the season without constant nurturing and care? In contrast, the wild flower—so delicate, so fragile, and often so rare—is rudely placed in conflict with all the raw elements of nature: drought, heat, cold, impoverished soil. And yet it survives these numbing forces, year after year, to the delight of everyone fortunate enough to gaze upon it.

More fundamentally, the author knew that by presenting his material in such a way he was playing upon a simple but nevertheless powerful psychological truth: Because of its universality, conflict strikes a responding chord in all humans, and in doing so causes the respondent to identify either directly or vicariously with the source, be this the writer (teacher) or his materials. There are of course other ingredients in drama—complexity, surprise, uncertainty, and a sense of awe, to name but a few. However, its most powerful component is the ability to induce conflict. A few writers of distinction, E. M. Forster among them, are strongly of the opinion that this special way of perceiving the world is for the most part unlearned and largely associated with creative ability. It is certainly not always associated with high intelligence or great powers of thought, since it is often found in persons without pretense to erudition. Nevertheless, it is sufficiently rare that the public is willing to pay huge sums of money for the privilege of entering vicariously into the unique experience it affords us.

Be this as it may, most teachers are totally bereft of any notion of how to achieve it. Nor are they aware that when, as students, they were themselves deeply moved by conceptual materials, the teacher or professor who stood before them was in all likelihood practicing a very similar strategy. As a consequence, I am sure that this ability is one of the true measures of giftedness among teachers.

Closely tied to the identification principle as it operates through dramatization are the strategies of reinforcement most notably promulgated in the theoretical works of B. F. Skinner.

Neo-Freudians are quick to point out the advantage of identification or modeling over reinforcement, an advantage which presumably lies in the fact that the former is a self-actuating process and therefore does not require reinforcement to induce affective learning. However, they do not quibble with the argument that both techniques, when used in conjunction, probably enhance learning and are in many instances so complementary in their functions as to become virtually inseparable. This is strongly apparent in the few studies of pupil/teacher interaction that show a significant relationship between teaching style and student attitudes and achievement. I refer specifically to the reports of researchers such as Donald M. Medley, Harold Mitzel,[136] W. W. Lewis, John Withall,[137] and Ned Flanders.[138] Basing the statement on his own experimental findings and those of other investigators, Flanders states unequivocally that

> ...the percentage of teacher statements that *make use of ideas and opinions previously expressed by pupils* is directly related to average class scores on attitude scales and teacher attractiveness, liking the class, etc., as well as to average achievement scores adjusted for initial ability.[139]

In reviewing several of his experiments, it is obvious that Professor Flanders was not interested in interpreting his data within a Freudian or Skinnerian context; he was content merely to show that when teachers adopted a certain teaching style, student attitudes and achievement are significantly affected. Nevertheless, the method at closer glance is subject to an important psychological interpretation: namely, that when interaction succeeds in the classroom, it succeeds only to the degree that reinforcement and identification are key operating factors. This is not to detract from its significance as a teaching device; it is simply to say that when interaction, which involves the employment of a very special kind of reinforcement, serves the ego needs of the child—in this case a need for the kind of recognition that enjoys high social status—it constitutes an important means of activating the identification principle, thus allowing reinforcement and identification to work hand in glove. The resulting condition is one that vividly brings to mind our own exposure to the outstanding teacher. More often than not— and without really knowing why—we left his classroom feeling a few feet taller than we actually are.

* * *

In this view of how social conscience may be developed in young children, I have tried perhaps too hard to tip the scale on the side of emotive techniques rather than rational processes. So be it. The world of pure intelligence has no answers to the irrefutable logic of Swift's *Modest Proposal.* It too easily condones the Auschwitz horror chambers, the charnel house at Hiroshima, and the napalm-ravaged children of Vietnam.

Besides, I can think of no other way of doing what so desperately needs to be done. During my years as a teacher, and in my daily visits to elementary and secondary classrooms, I have seen little to convince me that scholarly examinations of the great moral issues (the enslavement of blacks, for example) have been anything more than intellectual exercises. I cannot believe that you teach the values most deeply rooted in social experience by the construction of hypotheses, by field trips, or by the innocent mimicry of democratic processes.

Nor do I see any real hope in the *moral dilemmas* approach of Harvard's Lawrence Kohlberg or in the *values clarification* formula of Sidney B. Simon of the University of Massachusetts, both of whose packaged techniques are finding their way into American classrooms on a national scale. Ironically, the primary weakness of the moral dilemmas approach lies in its total dependence on rational processes. Although Kohlberg's data offer some evidence of increased moral awareness and the ability to reason morally, the fact remains that the link between moral reasoning and behaving morally is very weak if not virtually nonexistent. The alleged results of Simon's *values clarification* packet are even more debatable. In fact, I wonder if using the packet may not be morally dangerous. Here, the concept of "right" or "wrong" is utterly without meaning, because there is no such thing: stated values are accepted on an equal basis so long as they are accompanied by knowledge. This stance of moral neutrality cannot but lead children to believe that all values are equally valid, or that moral commitment, based on feeling or emotion, is far less important than one's ability to "talk" about morals. The fact that it offers teachers and school districts a refuge from the dangerous practice of adopting a moral position no doubt carries a certain attractiveness. As one critic has noted, this "principled amorality," which poses no threat to anyone, is without question the primary reason for its rapidly growing popularity within the public schools.[140]

To the degree that values can be taught at all, I believe you teach them by involving children emotionally in the lives of individuals and groups locked in struggles of significant moral consequence. When a child has felt something of the degradation of the black slave through empathy, when vicarious experience has set the iron barb of subjection deep into his own flesh—then, and only then—does he begin to internalize the attitudes that give flesh and blood to a value we call human equality. This is the work of the teacher who is first and foremost a dramatist and second a purveyor of knowledge—definitely in that order.

The primacy of literary truth still applies. Where children are concerned, our priorities are crystal clear. We must set the stage for them at an earlier age than we ever thought necessary before. Moreover, the drama to be enacted, borrowing equally from the vast record of man's inhumanity to man, must engage the heart even more than the mind. Its basic appeal, in short, must be emotional.

The advantage to this is as plain today as it was two thousand years ago when the Father sent his Only Begotten Child into the world, saying: "Remember, my Son, your adversary is a formidable logician with a breadth of knowledge next only to mine."

"I will play his game of chance," the Son of Man replied. He smiled cunningly as He spoke, fingering in the secret compartment of his robe a pair of loaded dice.

References

Chapter One

1. Quoted in the *Phi Delta Kappan,* May 1967, p. 418.
2. John H. Bunzell, "What's Happening to Democracy?" *Saturday Review,* May 17, 1969, pp. 28, 29.
3. Ibid., p. 28.
4. Ibid., p. 29.
5. Richard Hofstader, *Anti-intellectualism in American Life* (New York: Alfred A. Knopf, 1962). Read Chapter 14, pp. 359-90, titled "The Child and the World," for his development of this theme.
6. John Dewey, *How We Think* (New York: D.C. Heath, 1933).
7. John I. Goodlad, "Curriculum: The State of the Field," *Review of Educational Research,* June 1960, pp. 188, 189.
8. Reported in *Education U.S.A.,* Washington, D.C., September 18, 1967.
9. Joseph Wood Krutch, *The Measure of Man* (New York: Bobbs-Merrill, 1953), p. 79.
10. Gordon Allport, *The Nature of Prejudice* (Cambridge: Addison-Wesley, 1954), p. 488.
11. Ann E. Freedman, *The Planned Society: An Analysis of Skinner's Proposals* (Kalamazoo, Mich.: Behaviordella, 1972), p. 4.
12. Bertrand Russell, *A History of Western Philosophy* (New York: Simon and Schuster, 1945), p. 834.
13. Clyde Kluckhohn, *Culture and Behavior* (New York: Macmillan 1964), pp. 286-87.

Chapter Two

14. Bertrand Russell, *A History of Western Philosophy,* p. 828.
15. Theodore Brameld, *Cultural Foundations of Education* (New York: Harper & Brothers, 1957), p. 13.
16. From Jacob W. Getzels's chapter, "The Acquisition of Values in School and Society," in Francis S. Chase and Harold A. Anderson (eds.), *The High School in a New Era* (Chicago: University of Chicago Press, 1958), pp. 152-55.
17. From the chapter by W. W. Charters, Jr., titled "The Social Background of Teaching," in N. L. Gage (ed.), *Handbook of Research on Teaching* (Chicago: Rand McNally, 1963), pp. 727-30.
18. James P. Shaver, "Reflective Thinking, Values, and Social Studies Textbooks," *School Review,* Autumn 1965, p. 327.
19. Clarence H. Faust, "Theory and Practice of Education in the United States," in *Humanism and Education in East and West* (Paris: A Unesco Publication, 1953), p. 62.
20. Bertrand Russell, *A History of Western Philosophy,* p. 826.
21. Pitirim A. Sorokin, *The Reconstruction of Humanity* (Boston: Beacon Press, 1948), p. 104.
22. Edith West and William Gardner, "The Role of the Social Studies in Developing Values," Background Paper No. 11, (Social Studies Curriculum Development Center, University of Minnesota, 1968), p. 15.
23. *Bellevue American,* Bellevue, Washington, April 1, 1971, p. 1.

24. See John Bowlby's summary of these investigations entitled *Maternal Care and Mental Health* (Geneva: World Health Organization, Monograph Series No. 2, 1951).

25. Gordon W. Allport, *Becoming* (New Haven: Yale University Press, 1955), p. 33.

26. Ashley Montagu, *The Direction of Human Development* (New York: Harper & Brothers, 1955), p. 153.

27. Arthur Campbell Garnett, *The Moral Nature of Man* (New York: Ronald Press, 1952), p. 78.

Chapter Three

28. Joseph Wood Krutch, "A Humanist's Approach," *Phi Delta Kappan*, March 1970, p. 378.

29. Bertrand Russell, *The Problems of Philosophy* (London: Oxford University Press, 1967). See his chapter "Truth and Falsehood," pp. 119-31, for a complete discussion of the problem.

30. Rudolph Carnap in *The Age of Analysis*, edited by Morton White (New York: Mentor books, 1961), pp. 203-25.

31. Bertrand Russell, *A History of Western Philosophy*, p. 834.

32. Lawrence E. Metcalf and Maurice C. Hunt, *Teaching High School Social Studies* and *Theory and Practice of the Social Studies*, published in 1955 and 1956 respectively.

33. Lawrence E. Metcalf, "Research on Teaching the Social Studies," in N. L. Gage (ed.), *Handbook of Research on Teaching* (Chicago: Rand McNally, 1963).

34. See the definitive article by James P. Shaver, "Reflective Thinking, Values, and Social Studies Textbooks," *School Review*, Autumn 1966, pp. 319-31, in which Shaver credits Metcalf for his work in the field.

35. Lawrence E. Metcalf, "Some Guidelines for Changing Social Studies Education," *Social Education*, April 1963, p. 201.

36. Ibid.

37. John Bowlby, op. cit.

38. Desmond Morris, *The Naked Ape* (New York: Dell Publishing Co., 1969).

39. Konrad Lorenz, *On Aggression* (New York: Bantam Books, (1967)

40. Robert Ardrey, *African Genesis* (New York: Dell Publishing Co., 1969).

41. Desmond Morris, op. cit. p. 9. This theme generally persists throughout the book.

42. "Bertrand Russell on the Sinful Americans: A Somewhat Frustrating Exchange of Letters," *Harper's*, June 1963, pp. 20-26.

43. Lee J. Cronbach, *Educational Psychology* (New York: Harcourt, Brace & World, 1963), p. 449.

44. Edgar Z. Friedenberg, *The Vanishing Adolescent* (New York: Dell Publishing Co., 1969), p. 92.

Chapter Four

45. George S. Counts, "Dare Progressive Education Be Progressive?" *Progressive Education,* vol. 9, 1932, p. 263.

46. Ibid., pp. 257-63.

47. George S. Counts, *Dare the School Build a New Social Order?* (New York: John Day, 1936), p. 12.

48. Frank N. Magill (ed.), *Masterpieces of World Philosophy* (New York: Harper and Row, 1961), p. xvii.

49. Daniel Aaron, "The Radical Humanism of John Steinbeck," *Saturday Review,* September 28, 1968, p. 26.

50. John W. Aldridge, *After the Lost Generation* (New York: The Noonday Press, 1951), p. 135.

51. W. Somerset Maugham, *Books and You* (New York: Doubleday Doran, 1940), pp. 55, 56.

52. As an example of this, read Joseph P. Firebaugh, "The Pragmatism of Henry James," *Virginia Quarterly Review,* vol. 27, 1951, pp. 419-35.

53. Quoted in Henry Steele Commager's *Living Ideas in America* (New York: Harper & Brothers, 1951), p. 584.

54. Lee J. Cronbach, op. cit., pp. 452, 453.

55. Muzafer Sherif and Carolyn W. Sherif, *An Outline of Social Psychology* (New York: Harper and Brothers, 1956), p. 573.

56. Ibid., p. 560.

57. Max Savelle, *The Colonial Origins of American Thought* (New York: D. Van Nostrand, 1964), pp. 122, 123.

58. Lee J. Cronbach, op. cit., p. 448.

59. Ralph Linton, in Ruth Anshen (ed.), *Moral Principles of Action* (New York: Harper & Brothers, 1952), p. 646.

Chapter Five

60. Michael Crighton, *The Terminal Man* (New York: Alfred A. Knopf, 1972), pp. 242, 243.

61. Quoted from Urie Bronfenbrenner, *Two Worlds of Childhood* (New York: Russell Sage Foundation, 1970), p. xiii.

62. Ibid.

63. Ibid.

64. James S. Coleman, *The Adolescent Society* (New York: The Free Press of Glencoe, 1961), p. 9.

65. Urie Bronfenbrenner, op. cit., p. xv.

66. Max Savelle, op. cit., pp. 72, 73.

67. Ibid., p. 73.

68. Ibid., p. 74.

69. Ibid., p. 75, 76.

70. Ibid., p. 76.

71. Allan Nevins and Henry Steele Commager, *A Pocket History of the United States* (New York: Washington Square Press, 1969), p. 98.

72. Ibid., pp. 99-112.

73. This is a paraphrased but essentially correct statement from an

education special on Ohio's fiscal crisis televised by the NBC network in December 1977.

74. Eckhard H. Hess, *Imprinting* (New York: D. Van Nostrand, 1973), p. 37.

75. Ibid., p. 41.

76. Konrad Lorenz, *Motivation of Human and Animal Behavior* (New York: Van Nostrand Reinhold, 1973), p. 43.

77. Eckhard H. Hess, op. cit., p. 40.

78. Quoted from Bruno Bettelheim, *The Empty Fortress* (New York: The Free Press, 1967), p. 40.

79. Konrad Lorenz, *Motivation of Human and Animal Behavior,* pp. 42-44.

80. Eckhard H. Hess, op. cit., p. 55.

81. Ibid.

82. Ibid., p. 57

83. Ibid., p. 52.

84. Ibid.

85. Ibid., p. 383.

86. Bruno Bettelheim, *The Empty Fortress,* p. 416.

87. Ibid., p. 231.

88. Ibid., pp. 41, 42.

89. Ibid., p. 42.

90. Erik H. Erikson, *Childhood and Society* (New York: W. W. Norton, 1963), pp. 247-51.

91. Ibid., p. 239.

92. Henry W. Maier, *Three Theories of Child Development* (New York: Harper and Row, 1969), p. 38.

93. Ibid., p. 118.

94. Ibid., p. 188.

95. Jacob W. Getzels, op. cit.

96. Sigmund Freud, "The Dissection of the Psychical Personality," in *The Standard Edition of the Complete Psychological Works of Sigmund Freud,* vol. xxii (New York: W. W. Norton, 1961), pp. 57-80.

97. Konrad Lorenz, *Motivation of Human and Animal Behavior,* p. 53.

98. Bruno Bettelheim, *Love Is Not Enough* (New York: The Free Press, 1970), p. 37.

99. William H. Hartup and Nancy L. Smothergill (eds.), *The Young Child: Reviews of Research* (Washington, D.C.: National Association for the Education of Young Children, 1970), pp. 42-57.

100. Harry Waters, "What TV Does to Kids," *Newsweek,* February 21, 1977, p. 64.

101. Urie Bronfenbrenner, op. cit., p. 1.

102. Ibid., pp. 95-119.

103. Ibid., pp. 95-99.

104. Kenneth Keniston, "Do Americans Really Like Children?" *Today's Education,* November/December 1975, pp. 16-19.

105. Rolf E. Muuss, *Theories of Adolescence* (New York: Random House, 1962), pp. 34-36.

Chapter Six

106. Melford E. Spiro, *Children of the Kibbutz* (Cambridge: Harvard University Press, 1975).

107. Alfred Yale (ed.), *Grouping in Education* (New York: John Wiley & Sons, 1966), p. 70.

108. Marian Franklin Pope, "Multigrading in Elementary Education," *Childhood Education,* May 1967, p. 514.

109. Joseph S. Junell, "An Analysis of the Effects of Multigrading on a Number of Noncognitive Variables," Unpublished Dissertation (Seattle: University of Washington, 1971), pp. 19-35.

110. Lyn S. Martin and Barbara N. Pavan, "Current Research on Open Space, Nongrading, Vertical Grouping, and Team Teaching," *Phi Delta Kappan,* January 1976, pp. 310-15.

111. Joseph Junell, op. cit., p. 2.

112. Ibid.

113. Urie Bronfenbrenner, op. cit., pp. 121, 122.

114. William Golding, *Lord of the Flies* (New York: Coward-McCann, 1955).

115. Urie Bronfenbrenner, op. cit., p. 122.

116. Bruno Bettelheim, *The Children of the Dream* (New York: Macmillan, 1969).

117. Melford E. Spiro, op. cit.

118. As a preparation for any American educator about to initiate a preschool program, I strongly recommend a careful reading of Spiro's *Children of the Kibbutz* and Bettelheim's *The Children of the Dream,* along with Bronfenbrenner's *Two Worlds of Childhood.* Bronfenbrenner's book is still the most definitive treatment on Russian methods and techniques.

119. Melford E. Spiro, op. cit., p. xv.

120. Urie Bronfenbrenner, op. cit., p. 119.

121. Melford E. Spiro, op. cit., p. xv.

122. Kenneth Keniston, op. cit., p. 19.

123. Ibid.

124. Ibid.

125. Wilson C. Riles, "ECE in California Passes Its First Tests," *Phi Delta Kappan,* September 1975, pp. 3-7.

Chapter Seven

126. Robert Rosenthal, *Pygmalion in the Classroom* (New York: Holt, Rinehart, and Winston, 1968), p. 20.

127. N. L. Gage (ed.), *Handbook of Research on Teaching* (Chicago: Rand McNally, 1963), pp. 506-83.

128. Erich Fromm, *The Art of Loving* (New York: Bantam Books, Harper & Row, 1963), p. 98.

129. Robert Rosenthal, op. cit.

130. Urie Bronfenbrenner, op. cit. p. 154.

Chapter Eight

131. Gilbert Highet, *The Art of Teaching* (New York: Vintage Books, 1950), p. vii.

132. In my article titled "Is Rational Man Our First Priority?" (*Phi Delta Kappan*, November 1970, p. 150), I mentioned having looked carefully into a number of basic readers. I find, upon reexamination, that the situation has changed very little, if at all, in recent years.

133. Joseph S. Junell, *Exploring the Northwest* (Chicago: Follett, 1966), p. 16.

134. Ibid.

135. B. F. Skinner, *Beyond Freedom and Dignity* (New York: Bantam Vintage Books, 1972), pp. 41-45.

136. N. L. Gage (ed.), op. cit., pp. 247-329.

137. Ibid., pp. 683-715.

138. Robert L. Ebel, Victor H. Noll, and Roger M. Bauer (eds.), *Encyclopedia of Educational Research* (London: Macmillan, 1969), p. 1426.

139. Ibid.

140. Amitai Etzioni, "Can Schools Teach Kids Values?" *Today's Education*, September/October 1977, p. 32.